# God Submarines

Go Below the Waves of Urgency, Anxiety and Heartbreak Using These Simple Tools to Deepen Your Relationship With God.

By: Timothy Jemly

©2019 All Rights Reserve

Copyright © 2019 by Timothy Jemly

**God's Submarines** / by Timothy Jemly

All rights reserved. No part of this publication may be reproduced, distributed or transmitted in any form or by any means, including photocopying, recording, or other electronic or mechanical methods, without the prior written permission of the publisher, except in the case of brief quotations embodied in critical reviews and certain other noncommercial uses permitted by copyright law.

Although the author and publisher have made every effort to ensure that the information in this book was correct at press time, the author and publisher do not assume and hereby disclaim any liability to any party for any loss, damage, or disruption caused by errors or omissions, whether such errors or omissions result from negligence, accident, or any other cause.

Adherence to all applicable laws and regulations, including international, federal, state and local governing professional licensing, business practices, advertising, and all other aspects of doing business in the US, Canada or any other jurisdiction is the sole responsibility of the reader and consumer

# Dedication

To my amazing wife Amber. Without whom I wouldn't be able to accomplish even half the things that I do. Your cheerful, giving nature inspires me to be a better person and to continually pursue God. No disrespect to the rest of you ladies, but Amber is the best wife in the whole world. Thanks to her love and support I am able to fulfill the calling God has on my life. She believes in me, even when I don't believe in myself, and she reminds me to look to God when I start to become discouraged. Thank you Amber, for the love, encouragement and hours spent watching our baby while I worked on this book.

# Contents

Free Bonus Gift ...................................................................7

Introduction ........................................................................9

Diving Deep with God .......................................................15

Meditation: Adjusting the antenna ..................................21

Dream and Vision Work ...................................................35

Get an "A" in Bible Class .................................................43

Fasting – Feasting in the Spirit .......................................53

Confession: Not just for Catholics ..................................63

The Fellowship of the Trinity ..........................................73

Prayer: Spiritual Air .........................................................83

Simple Simplicity .............................................................95

The Sub Mission ............................................................107

Sabbath ..........................................................................119

Putting it all together ....................................................131

Make a Difference .........................................................141

About the Author ..........................................................143

# Free Bonus Gift

This book is part of a larger curriculum I have developed to help you grow in your relationship with God. The entire training, in video format, normally sells for $29.95. Because I want to make sure you get the most out of this book, I am offering it to you free of charge. To receive your free videos please visit:

https://www.subscribepage.com/submarines

# ✱✱✱

# Introduction

Is your spiritual life stuck like a cat in a milk carton? Would your family describe you as a squirrel on speed — rushing from one urgent task to another? Life comes at us so fast that it is hard to find time for what is truly important. When is the last time you sat and had a leisurely conversation with your family or friends? If there was a contest for worrying, would you be a top competitor? Do the stresses of money and the demands of others constantly chew on the corners of your brain? Are you caught in survival mode — just trying to make it through another day? Do you want to enjoy life, but you just can't find the time? You may be one major crisis away from a nervous breakdown.

Or perhaps life is pretty good. Like Charlie Sheen you would say you are "winning at life", but you can't shake the feeling there should be something more. Everything is surface level. There is no anchor, no deep meaning to your life; you know God should be that for you, but you just aren't fully experiencing it. If you allow yourself to slow down and think about it, you would say that your life doesn't have the richness you always imagined for yourself.

*Introduction*

If any of this describes you, then keep reading! I guarantee that if you will implement the concepts presented in this book, your life will be fuller, richer and more connected with God and your loved ones. No, the piles of laundry won't magically fold themselves. The trove of emails won't automatically be answered. Your kids won't suddenly be able to take care of themselves. You won't be immune from tragic accidents, sudden illness or the death of a loved one, but you can enjoy peace and joy in the midst of those things.

The unfolded laundry and the crying baby are like the small waves of the ocean. They aren't overwhelming, but they never stop. The tragic accidents and sudden illnesses are major hurricanes that can cause total destruction in your life. You can't avoid either of those things, but you can learn to live in the depths, below the waves so that you enjoy tranquility in the middle of even the worst storms. If you put these tools to use, you will find yourself so rooted in God that neither the everyday challenges nor the major storms have any effect on your mental or emotional state.

I have been teaching these tools for over ten years, but I have been living them even longer. I recently went through a particularly tough storm, and these tools helped me to stay joyful in what otherwise would have been a dark period in my life. Almost two years ago, I fell over twenty feet while rock climbing. I broke my hip, several ribs and my left arm. I was not allowed to put any weight on my hip for three months. I couldn't use crutches or a regular walker because of my broken arm. I had to use a specially designed walker that attached to my upper arm just to get to the bathroom. Almost two years later, I still can't walk without a limp. I love playing sports but I am unable to participate in them. I wasn't able to work for three months and I easily could have slipped into discouragement and depression.

Instead, I found that this trial has brought me closer to God and I have been able to maintain a positive and hope-filled attitude. There have been times during the last couple of years when discouragement began to creep into my life, but each time, God has spoken to my heart and renewed my joy. I credit that to God's grace and the tools He has taught me that help me to key in to His voice when I need it the most.

This climbing accident was not the first major storm in my life. When I was a teenager, my mom passed away from cancer. That tore my world apart, but it also brought me into a closer relationship with God than I had ever experienced before. My parents had done a good job of teaching me how to know God for myself, but when my

*Introduction*

mom died, I began a quest to find ways to know Him even better. It was this journey that led me to all the tools I am sharing in this book. As a pastor, I have seen this same pattern occur in many other people's lives. I have walked with many people through trials that could have ruined them, but instead I saw them grow stronger and closer to God.

There are other people, however, who completely fall apart and turn their backs on God when their life gets hard. I ask myself what the difference is? What I have observed is that those who have been deepening their relationship with God are driven even deeper when a storm hits. On the other hand, those who fall apart have only developed a shallow relationship with God. They seemed to truly love and trust God, but they never really spent the time to grow deep in His love. Jesus said it this way:

*"But everyone who hears these words of mine and does not put them into practice is like a foolish man who built his house on sand. The rain came down, the streams rose, and the winds blew and beat against that house, and it fell with a great crash"* Matthew 7:26-27 (NIV)

Putting Jesus' words into practice is really what this book is about. Every Christian wants to put His words into practice, but there are two things that tend to get in the way of that. One of those obstacles is simply not knowing how to do it. Many people have, at best, only been taught one or two ways to connect with God. The other major problem is busyness. Too many people are so overwhelmed with their to-do list that they can't seem to find the time to seek God. This book will help you with both of these issues. We will look at new ways to connect with God that you may never have thought of as well as how to rest and recharge.

    Sometimes, no matter how hard you try to simplify your life, things just seem to mount up and overwhelm you. I have been going through that very thing in my own life. Six months ago, we adopted a newborn baby girl. She had colic for the first three months, which, for the uninitiated, basically meant that she screamed inconsolably most of the night. She was born with some health conditions that prevented her from eating properly so she had to be fed every hour. In order to survive, my wife and I have had to start sleeping in shifts. Blessedly, the colic has passed and the feedings have lengthened to every three hours, but sleeping through the night still isn't happening.

*Introduction*

I learned very quickly that my normal routine for seeking God just wasn't able to happen during this season of my life. However, every night I have to awaken several times to feed my baby. It usually takes 30 minutes to an hour or more to get her back to sleep. I have started using that time for prayer, meditation and sacred imagination. My devotional life doesn't look like what it did before, but because I know how to utilize many different tools, my spiritual life continues to grow.

In this book I pass on to you the knowledge I have been blessed with so that you too can enjoy a deeper relationship with your Maker, regardless of what is going on in your life. The submarines discussed in this book aren't a magic pill that will instantly transform you as you read about them. They are tools that you must put to work, but when you do, your life will change. I promise you that if you will put these concepts into practice and stay with them, one year from now your relationship with God will be stronger and deeper than you ever imagined possible. So, turn the page and let's get started today!

# 1
# Diving Deep with God

Do you ever feel like you are caught in an endless round of activity and that no matter how hard you try you are never able to catch up? I saw a sign one time that read *"God put me on earth to accomplish a certain number of things and right now I am so far behind that I'm never going to die."*

Does this describe you? Are you so overworked and busy that when you do sit down to spend some time with God, you immediately fall asleep? You thought you saw the light at the end of the tunnel once, but it turned out it was a train's headlight and it just ran you over. Now you are so tired, beat down, overwhelmed and discouraged you don't know which way to turn.

You look forward to vacation hoping that you will finally be able to relax and unwind, but you try to pack in all the fun you haven't had time for and end up needing a vacation from your vacation. You come back more stressed out than when you left and all your work has piled up while you were gone. Perhaps this verse in Isaiah 57:20-21 describes you. *"But the wicked are like the tossing sea, which cannot rest, whose waves cast up mire and mud. 'There is no peace,' says my God, for the wicked."* (KJV)

Wait a minute, you say! I'm not wicked; I'm a Christian. I've been born again. That's great, but have you then grown up or are you still a spiritual baby? Ephesians tells us that those who are spiritual infants are subject to the waves just like the wicked.

We will look at that text, but first, let's think about what it means to live your life in the shallows. The ocean is constantly in motion. The waves change size. When there is a hurricane there can be some real monsters. Other times the waves are manageable, but they never stop. If you live your life in the shallows, you are going to be in constant motion, constant unrest, and constant chaos. The waves pick up dirt and debris; in the same way, all the emotional baggage of our life is constantly being brought to the surface and rehashed.

In the last few years, I have developed sea sickness. I don't know why. I never used to get it at all, but now I do. I keep going out on the ocean though because I love both SCUBA diving and snorkeling. There is something odd that I've noticed. When I start to get seasick and we stop to dive or snorkel, I get worse when I snorkel, but better when I dive. That's because when I am snorkeling, I am still on the surface and I still feel the motion of the ocean. But when I dive, I go below the waves down deep where it is always calm, no matter how things are on the surface.

Psalm 42:7 says: "*Deep calls to deep, in the roar of Your waterfalls; all your waves and breakers have swept over me.*" God dwells in the depths and he has put within us a deep longing that cries out for him, under all our busyness is a longing for the stillness of the deep.

The last part of that verse says, "...your waves and breakers have swept over me." That carries a different connotation than being tossed by the waves. If the waves sweep over you then you are below them.

The United States Navy tells its submarine captains that in the event of an approaching hurricane, they are to head straight for the nearest spot where they can dive into the depths. Why? Because even in the biggest hurricane, things are calm down in the depths. It's like the song in The Little Mermaid says, "darling it's better, down where it's wetter, under the sea."

When you are in the shallows, it seems like there is never any break. One crisis after another hits you — some big and some small but you just never get a chance to slow down. Just as you are starting to recover from the last wave, the next one hits. Sometimes several hit you in rapid succession and you feel like you are drowning. These waves might be waves of busyness and stress, emotional waves, financial problems, health problems, temptations or a myriad of other things. But the point is, if you are hoping things are going to get better and that the waves will stop some day, you are going to be disappointed.

The surface of the ocean is never really calm. However, when you dive deep, it is always calm. One of the things I love about SCUBA diving is that it is impossible to move fast. You can't move quickly underwater; you have to take it slow. Not only that, but everything underwater seems to move at a leisurely pace (except for the rare moment when you see something get scared.) Even things that move fast, like dolphins, seem to do so effortlessly and without any sense of hurry.

So how do we get there spiritually? What are the spiritual equivalents to SCUBA gear, or even better yet, submarines that can stay submerged indefinitely? Ephesians 4:12-14 says "...*that the body of Christ may be built up until we all reach unity in the faith and in the knowledge of the Son of God and become mature, attaining to the whole measure of the fullness of Christ. Then we will no longer be infants, tossed back and forth by the waves, and blown here and there by every wind of teaching and by the cunning and craftiness of men in their deceitful scheming.*"

According to this verse, we will not be tossed around by the sea when we become like Jesus. Therefore, the things that help us go into the depths with God are the things that will help us to be like Jesus. They are the submarines.

I hope that I am not making you think that there is anything you could do to make yourself like Jesus. That is a work that God must do in you. However, just as we plant, water, fertilize and weed our gardens in order to allow God to work the miracle of making them grow, in the same way the submarines are things we do that prepare our hearts for God to work the miracle of growth in our life.

In each of the succeeding chapters of this book, we will examine a different submarine. These are the things that we can do to put ourselves in God's presence so that He can change us. Each of these are submarines in their own right; just doing that one thing will bring you closer to God. Paradoxically, all of the submarines are also part of a larger submarine. If you use all the submarines together, they form a larger submarine that will take you even deeper with God. Each of these submarines has a specific role to play in the larger submarine. For example, the submarine of prayer is like the oxygen supply on a submarine. Prayer should be as constant and natural as breathing. So, in going deep with God prayer represents the oxygen supply.

One final caution before we dive into the submarines. This book will do you no good if all you do is read it. These submarines are meant to be used; knowing about a submarine isn't the same things as diving deep in a submarine. I recommend that after reading each chapter you spend a week trying out the submarine before you go on to the next chapter.

You could spend your whole life trying to master just one of these submarines and not do it, but don't let that discourage you. You must remember that the point isn't to master the submarine, but to get to know God better. God promises that if you seek Him, you will find Him. So, I can say with certainty that if you learn these subs as a means to seek God, you will find Him!

# 2

# Meditation: Adjusting the antenna

I saw one of those endlessly forwarded Facebook stories recently that seems worth repeating. I was unable to determine if it is true or not, or what its original source was, but let's not let the facts get in the way of good story. It said something like:

Many years ago, before the age of cell phone and the internet, a man walked into a telegraph station to apply for a job as a telegraph operator. He was told to wait with seven other applicants who had arrived before him. He sat down for a couple of minutes and then got up and walked right past the receptionist into the inner offices. The boss came out a few minutes later and told the other applicants to go home because the position had been filled. This nearly created a riot as the job seekers exploded about the unfairness of hiring someone who should have been behind them in line, but just rudely barged in without waiting to be called. The boss then explained to them that the telegraph machine had been ticking out the following message the whole time: "*If you understand this message, come on back. The job is yours.*"

God is constantly telegraphing us messages. Do you receive and understand them? Fortunately, there is a tool that can help us to practice our spiritual Morse code. It is the submarine of meditation. Unfortunately, it is one of the most misunderstood and poorly used disciplines in the church today. When the average evangelical Christian hears the word meditation, the first thing that comes to mind is either a Buddhist monk levitating and repeating the word "ommm", or a Catholic nun sitting in a convent somewhere staring at a blank wall.

In fact, whenever someone starts teaching about meditation, they are inevitably accused of bringing "pagan" practices into the church. But the Bible makes repeated references to meditation. Joshua 1:8 commands us to meditate on the law day and night. Philippians 4:8 says "*Finally, brethren, whatever things are true, whatever things are noble, whatever things are just, whatever things are pure, whatever things are lovely, whatever things are of good report, if there is any virtue and if there is anything praiseworthy—meditate on these things.*" (KJV)

Some of you are probably used to hearing this text in the NIV which says think on these things. That's what meditation means—to think deeply about something. I am going to teach you how to do that. But I should warn you that some of the methods appear at first glance to be like the ones used by Buddhist monks. After all, their form of meditation is, I believe, a counterfeit. A good counterfeit is like the real thing. But you wouldn't go home and throw away all your money because there were counterfeit bills being circulated around town. No, you would go and find out how to tell the difference.

Imagine if the church treated prayer the way it has meditation. What if prayer had fallen into even more disuse than it has, and when someone tried to teach on prayer they were attacked because what they were talking about sounded like Islam. I can just hear the critics saying: "Don't Muslims pray five times a day?" "What do you mean I should bow my head, that's an Islamic teaching that we should bow in submission to Allah." This isn't as farfetched as it sounds. Even though prayer has always played an important role in the church, I have met evangelical Christians who believe that kneeling to pray is wrong because the "Catholics" do it.

*Meditation: Adjusting the antenna*

Please don't make the mistake of not doing something just because some other group of people does or doesn't do it. Our standard of behavior should be the Bible and nothing else. Psalm 46:10 says *"Be still, and know that I am God..."* Learning how to be still and wait for God is what meditation is about. Isaiah 40:31 promises, "They that wait upon the LORD shall renew their strength; they shall mount up with wings as eagles; they shall run, and not be weary; and they shall walk, and not faint." (KJV) Do you want to soar on eagle's wings? Would you like to be able to run and never get tired? Or maybe swim effortlessly like the dolphins, floating joyfully in the depths? You need this submarine.

Psalm 1:1-3 says: *"Blessed is the man who does not walk in the counsel of the wicked or stand in the way of sinners or sit in the seat of mockers. But his delight is in the law of the LORD, and on his law, he meditates day and night. He is like a tree planted by streams of water, which yields its fruit in season and whose leaf does not wither. Whatever he does prospers."*

Have you ever seen a tree that was in a hurry or was stressed out? That's silly, you say. A tree couldn't go anywhere; it's rooted in the ground. So of course, it can't hurry. But did you know that God wants you to be rooted down too? Not into the ground but into Him. Colossians 2:6,7 says: *"So then, just as you received Christ Jesus as Lord, continue to live in him, rooted and built up in him, strengthened in the faith as you were taught, and overflowing with thankfulness."*

So how do we root ourselves in Jesus? By doing what Psalms 1 tells us to do, meditating on His law (His Word) day and night. In other words, we are constantly thinking about Him all the time. But how in the world do you do that? I mean we have a million other things that are crying for our attention. We must work, and interact with other people, and do all kinds of things that require us to think about other things. So how could we possibly be thinking about the things of God all the time?

Deuteronomy 6:4-9 gives us a clue. It says: *"Hear, O Israel: The LORD our God, the LORD is one! You shall love the LORD your God with all your heart, with all your soul, and with all your strength. And these words which I command you today shall be in your heart. You shall teach them diligently to your children, and shall talk of them when you sit in your house, when you walk by the way, when you lie down, and when you rise up. You shall bind them as a sign on your hand, and they shall be as frontlets between your eyes. You shall write them on the doorposts of your house and on your gates."* (NIV) What

God is saying is that we should put reminders of scripture everywhere and try to make it the center of our life.

But how can you really be thinking about God all the time? Well, have you ever gotten a song stuck in your head that you just can't stop singing, and it's constantly playing in the back of your mind no matter what you are doing? What if you could replace that song with scripture? One method of meditation can help you to do that.

This method is tied to scripture memorization. I have often said that the most common way that I hear from God is through the scripture verses He puts in my mind that I have previously memorized. The goal of meditation is hearing from God, so it's not surprising that scripture memorization would be part of this experience. Choose a passage of scripture that is meaningful to you and begin memorizing it. There are a lot of different methods to memorizing scripture; experiment and find what works for you.

The last step in most memorization methods is to repeat what you have learned out loud 10 or 12 times. The reason for this is that your mind is like a dense forest; when you first hear a concept or think of a new idea it is like blazing a trail in that forest. Each time you think that idea again, you wear the path a little wider. If you say it out loud, it widens it even more. If you don't come back to that idea, the forest starts to grow back across the path. Therefore, you must come back and periodically review things you have memorized. If you're really dense, you have to come back really often.

But our goal isn't just to memorize scripture; we want it to replace that song that is stuck in our head all day. To do that, we must know why that song got stuck in our head in the first place. Firstly, music itself seems to widen the pathway in our brains. I can often hear a song once or twice and can remember the lyrics several days later. Secondly, the song is usually a repetitive song. I might only have listened to the song once, but in that one time, I heard the chorus repeated ten times. Thirdly, it usually has a catchy tune so I find myself singing it, and every time I do, that pathway is widening in my brain and making it more likely that I will sing it again. When you relax your mind and stop forcing it to concentrate on whatever you are doing now, your thoughts will automatically flow down the path of least resistance and you will find yourself thinking about whatever you usually think about most.

So, we can change our thoughts by simple repetition. Find a quiet, comfortable spot. Get your journal and a pen so that you can write down any impressions that you get from God. Sit up straight and repeat out loud the scripture you memorized. Try and do this about a hundred times. Your mind will scream against this kind of boring repetition. Your brain is going to tell you that this is a waste of time, that it is useless, that you aren't doing anything productive. When you start to get these thoughts, it is a sign that you know the scripture well enough that you can say it while thinking about other things. That is your cue to begin meditating on the passage.

Ask God questions about the passage and how He wants you to apply it to your life. Be sure to write down any responses you hear from Him. Keep repeating the scripture while you are doing this. At some point, you may find that repeating the scripture is becoming a distraction from hearing God's voice. When that happens simply stop and listen to God. If, after a few minutes, you find your mind has wandered on to other things, begin repeating the scripture passage again. The whole point of this exercise is to try and make the pathway in your brain so large that when your mind drifts, it drifts to the scripture.

Let's use Romans 12:2 as an example. This passage says: *"Do not conform any longer to the pattern of this world, but be transformed by the renewing of your mind. Then you will be able to test and approve what God's will is—his good, pleasing and perfect will."* (NIV) Once you have memorized this passage, you would begin to repeat it out loud over and over again.

When your mind starts to complain or drift to other things you would ask God to show you any areas of your life where you are conforming to the world. When you hear him tell you things you need to work on, write them down. Then you might ask God to show you what areas of your mind still needed to be renewed, what thoughts you have that aren't pleasing to him. As soon as these thoughts come to mind, it is going to be easy to slip into thinking them instead of meditating. Ask God to help you overcome them and go back to repeating the verse. Then, you might ask God to show you what His will is for you that day. Hopefully, throughout the day, this verse will come into your head, and when it does, it will remind you of the things God spoke to you as His will for today and help you to stay focused on the right things.

This is the point where some of you are saying, "Wait a minute. What you are talking about is a mantra; you are teaching transcendental meditation." No. I admit there are some similarities but there are also some differences. The differences are the differences between a counterfeit and the real thing. In transcendental meditation, they repeat a specific word or mantra repeatedly. The most well-known mantra is "ommm." The goal of this form of meditation is to blank out your mind and get rid of all thought. That is why they use a word like "ommm." The idea is that if you blank out your mind, you will be able to get in touch with your "higher self".

The idea of the Christian meditation I just described, on the other hand, is not to blank out your mind, but to focus it on the Word of God and ultimately on God Himself. The goal is to learn to know God as Himself. Not to know about God. Not to know God's blessings, not to know His word, not just to recognize His creation, or His work in my life, but to know Him as a person.

This is hard because sin has separated us from God and created a thick cloud that makes it difficult for us to experience God. Most of the time we settle for experiencing His creation, or we settle for experiencing His Word, and certainly God speaks to us through these things. However, we find examples of people in scripture such as Enoch and Moses who spoke with God face to face. They pierced the cloud of sin and were able to know God as He really is.

2 Corinthians 3:17-18 says: "*And we, who with unveiled faces all reflect the Lord's glory, are being transformed into his likeness with ever-increasing glory, which comes from the Lord, who is the Spirit*".(NIV) After Moses talked with God, his face would glow and He would wear a veil so that the people wouldn't see the glory slowly fading from his face. But we are to constantly be in God's presence and with unveiled faces, we are to reflect God's glory to the world.

Since the goal of meditation is to know God personally, the way of setting about doing that is going to be as unique and varied as the individuals meditating. There is no one way to meditate; you must find what works for you. I am merely giving you a starting point for your journey. If you find that what I just talked about isn't a good starting point for you, let me offer you another idea. Genesis 6:5 tells us that during the time of Noah, God looked at the earth and God saw that the wickedness of man was great in the earth and that every imagination of the thoughts of his heart was only evil continually. Let me ask you: What is the imagination of your heart like? What do you daydream about? What do your thoughts drift to when you let your mind wander? God gave you your imagination and He intended you to use it for good.

Kids have great imaginations and they use them for all sorts of things. But by the time we become adults, most of us only use our imagination to imagine fulfilling our greed, our lusts, or our egos. Ask yourself how many of your daydreams involve you winning the lottery, dating a supermodel, or doing some great thing that brings you accolades. If that describes most of your daydreams, then God would say that the imaginations of your heart are only evil continually.

It won't do any good to try not thinking about those things. That will only make the pathway that much wider in your brain. You need to replace them with new and better dreams. Try this. Find a comfortable place to sit. Read a story from the Bible. Then close your eyes, and imagine you are one of the characters in the story. Try to incorporate as many details as possible; it's OK to add things if they don't change the gist of the story. Try to incorporate all your senses. What do you smell, feel, taste, see and hear?

Don't rush this experience. Try to make it play out in real time like a movie in your mind. For example, maybe you are imagining being a disciple in the boat when Jesus calmed the storm.

We can read that passage in under a minute, but to have lived it would have been a several hour ordeal. In the movie version, this would probably be a fifteen-minute scene. That is the version you want to go for — the fifteen-minute movie version. After you have finished imagining the scene, then invite God to speak to you and show you what He wants you to learn from that passage of scripture.

Your mind may wander to other things several times when you are first learning to do this. You must discipline your mind. Your mind has years of pathways worn imagining evil; it is going to take time to for the new pathways to become wider than the old ones. But keep at it, and eventually, you may find yourself daydreaming about heaven as you fold the laundry or do paperwork at the office. That, in turn, can lead you into a personal knowledge of God.

Many Christians know a lot about God and His Word, but that isn't what God wants. God wants us to know Him. Thanks to the paparazzi, I know a lot about Paris Hilton, but I don't know her at all. In the same way, it is possible to know a lot about God and even to know the Bible well and not know God at all.

A few years ago, there was a professional actor who toured the country reciting Psalm 23 for live audiences. Everywhere he went, he got standing ovations. But at one location a young man got up and asked if he could recite the poem instead. The actor was taken aback, but agreed to let the boy have a chance. When he was done, the entire audience was weeping. The actor was amazed and asked the young man how, with so little acting experience, he could move the audience so profoundly. The young man replied, "You know the Psalm; I know the shepherd".i

Do you know the shepherd? If not, perhaps now would be a good time to put down this book and spend some time getting to know Him.

# 3
# Dream and Vision Work

I have a mental spot where I often go to meet with God as I meditate. It is a natural hot spring on a mountain top. The views are amazing and I often have great conversations with God there. He teaches me amazing things about the Bible and life. Some would say it isn't a real place, as I get there through my imagination. But the Spirit told me that anywhere I meet Him is more real than any place I have seen or touched.

2 Corinthians 4:18 says: *"so we fix our eyes not on what is seen, but on what is unseen, since what is seen is temporary, but what is unseen is eternal."* So even though I can't see it with my waking eyes, I believe the place where I meet God is eternal and more real than my living room.

One day, we were in this special place looking up at the clouds and playing a little game where we form the clouds into various objects. (God doesn't just look at the clouds and decide what they look like He actively forms them into things, and He taught me how to do that as well.) I had been praying a lot at that time that

God would help me to pursue Him wholeheartedly. Suddenly, Jesus jumped up and said, "So you want to pursue me? Let's see if you can keep up." He formed a motorcycle out of the clouds and jumped on and took off. I said, "Oh yeah" and I formed a rocket to chase Him. Unfortunately, my rocket wouldn't turn and I shot out toward space.

I quickly formed a jet to bring me back and let me chase Him, but even that wouldn't corner tight enough, so I formed another motorcycle to chase Him with. Soon we were racing along a winding road next to steep cliffs that dropped off into the ocean. I rounded a sharp bend and found the road covered with livestock. I jammed on the brakes and tried to avoid them, but inevitably crashed. Jesus came back and healed me and helped me up.

I said, "*Jesus did you put those animals there on purpose?*" He smiled and said "*I wanted to see if you had the faith to jump them. Come on; we aren't done.*" With that, He turned and jumped off the cliff into the water. I followed Him and soon found myself diving deep into the ocean. The water got darker and darker until I couldn't see anything. The Spirit told me to hold my breath in the natural realm as I was imagining this, and soon I felt like my lungs would burst. Then Jesus appeared with a fish that had a strange light on its head that allowed us to see. Jesus also had a rebreather, which He handed me and I gratefully began to breathe again.

We continued downward until we entered a cave and then angled up and the water fell away as we came up in an underwater cavern filled with precious jewels. Jesus said, "This is my treasure room; go ahead and have a look around." I stood amazed and slowly looked around. I saw a red jewel among the others that seemed to draw my attention. I picked it up and looked deeply into it. Jesus said, "That one is called Salvation."

I stood transfixed looking at it. In the center of the stone, I could see Jesus hanging on the cross. I instantly understood His sacrifice and the truth of Salvation in a deeper way than I ever had before. I continued to stare at the stone for a long time. My heart learned more about salvation than I could have in months of study on the subject. I understood it in a way that goes deeper than words can describe.

There is much more to this adventure, and there are many other adventures I could write about. But this is not a book of my personal exploits with God. I share this experience to help give you an understanding of the kind of relationship I believe that God wants to have with each of us. God wants to have an intimate relationship with you. But the truth is, it is very difficult for us to experience intimacy with someone we can't see, hear or feel. I believe that God gave humanity two things as a backup method for us to experience intimacy with Him if we ever were cut off from His presence by sin. Those two things are dreams and our imagination.

The second half of this chapter will be devoted to dreams, but let's consider our imaginations for a moment. How do you use your imagination? When you were a child, I bet you imagined all kinds of things. As an adult, most people seldom use their imaginations, and when they do they are mostly fantasizing about fulfilling their sexual fantasies, winning the lottery, or taking revenge on the guy who cut them off in traffic. Other people are anxious all the time because they allow their imagination to dwell on all the terrible things that could go wrong. But God commands us not to be anxious. All these ways of using our imagination are what God would call evil.

Have you ever considered the reasons God gave for condemning the people who lived before the flood? Genesis 6:5 says: "*And God saw that the wickedness of man was great in the earth, and that every imagination of the thoughts of his heart was only evil continually.*" (KJV) Part of His condemnation was that they only used their imagination for evil instead of using it to connect with Him.

Some Christians I know are scared of their imaginations. They are afraid that the devil or even their own hearts will deceive them and lead them astray. It's true that we need to carefully test any direction and truth that comes to us through our imagination. However, the primary way that God uses our imagination isn't to teach us truth or even to give us direction. The real power of our imagination is to intertwine our hearts with His. We could get all the truth and direction we need from God through other sources, but if we aren't connecting with God through our imagination, our hearts are going to be empty and cold. Meet God today in your imagination and let Him warm your heart.

Joel 2:28 says: *"And afterward, I will pour out my Spirit on all people. Your sons and daughters will prophesy, your old men will dream dreams, your young men will see visions."* (NIV) Peter proclaimed in the book of Acts that beginning at Pentecost, this prophecy is fulfilled. That means that from the time of the early church until now, this should have been our normal experience. I was pondering this and realized that using your imagination is a form of spiritual vision. Now, I certainly wouldn't argue that it is the only form. I am certain that God appears to people in supernatural ways that are beyond our normal experience. But what if the Spirit's work in our lives that might prepare us for these greater encounters has been hampered by our unwillingness to use our imaginations as God intended?

This got me thinking about dreams. I always imagined that if I had a dream from God, Jesus would appear in the dream as a glowing figure and would give me instructions on what I need to do. I began to wonder: What if the dreams I have regularly that I attributed to eating pizza late at night were actually God speaking to me?

I looked to the Bible for examples of the kinds of dreams I should expect. What I found was surprising. There were a couple of examples of Jesus, or an angel, showing up directly in a dream and telling the dreamer what to do. But most of the dreams recorded in scripture were things that I would have dismissed as a pizza dream. Birds eat bread out of a basket on a guy's head; some skinny cows eat some fat cows; the sun, moon, and stars bow down and worship the dreamer, and a bunch of crazy looking animals walk out of the ocean. All these dreams were symbolic, not literal. The difference between their dreams and mine was these biblical dreamers believed that the dreams were from God and wouldn't rest until they had an interpretation.

If God is speaking in symbolic language, then we need a key for understanding it. Therefore, I began setting about to learn how to interpret dreams. I tried several different things, but one of the most helpful resources I have found is a book by Dr. Mark Virkler and Charity Virkler Kayembe called "Hearing God Through Your Dreams." If you are serious about learning to hear God's voice through your dreams, I highly recommend this book. I will give you the basic outline of their method here just to whet your appetite.

The first thing you must know about your dream is the setting. What were you thinking about when you went to bed? What have you been praying about recently? What has been weighing heavily on your mind and heart? This is the setting for the dream.

The next question to ask is what is the primary action in the dream? Are you searching, hiding, running, questioning? Then, ask: What is the primary emotion in the dream. Are you fearful, excited, happy, angry? Now consider where in your waking life you are experiencing this emotion, and where you are performing this action. Ask the Holy Spirit to guide you and then overlay the dream on the waking life situation that you see these actions and emotions lining up with. Soon you will begin to see what the different aspects of your dream are symbolizing. Once you have the symbols clear, the message God is giving you about that situation will begin to emerge. Take some time to journal about your dream and listen for the Holy Spirit's voice as He speaks to you about the situation He first brought up with you in your dream.

    Set this book down for a moment and just let the truth of God's love for you soak in for a moment. He loves you so much that He is willing to meet you in your dreams and imagination. His presence isn't something we are just imagining; he is actually there! Someday we will awaken to a higher reality and Sleeping Beauty's story will be ours. We will sing to our prince "I know you, I walked with you once upon a dream." Until then, dreams and visions can be a powerful submarine to help us go deep with God and get out of the churning chaos of our lives.

# 4
# Get an "A" in Bible Class

I love it when they have a Bible category on "Jeopardy." It is the only time when I know all the answers. Actually, it's Jeopardy so it's technically the only time I know all the questions. But I digress. It's not because I have been to seminary and spent all these years studying biblical exegesis, which allows me to come up with the correct response every time. It's that they make the questions so easy that I would have been able to answer all of them when I was in first grade.

But what amazes me is they give an answer like "He is famous for building an ark" and the players, who just successfully came up with the correct question for the answer "He won the Academy award for best actor in 1963," don't have a clue. Over 80% of the population of this country profess to be Christians, but biblical literacy in this country is at an all-time low. People profess to serve God, but they don't know anything about Him.

Deuteronomy 8:3 says: *"Man does not live on bread alone, but on every word that comes from the mouth of the LORD."* (NIV) This means that studying scripture is the way that we feed our spiritual nature. So, if we have a bunch of Christians out there who don't know their Bibles, then they are spiritually starving. There are some species of birds that regurgitate their food for their babies to eat. It really is pretty disgusting when you think about it. But there are some Christians who never study for themselves; the only spiritual food they get is what has already been pre-digested for them by a pastor. They're like little baby birds saying, "Feed me, feed me."

Don't get me wrong; I am not saying that memorizing a bunch of facts about God and knowing your Bible inside and out is what is going to save you. But the Bible is God's letter to you. If you love Him, wouldn't you want to read and study it regularly?

Let me explain it another way. Suppose you had a friend who tells you he's getting married. You congratulate him and ask him what his soon-to-be bride's name is and he doesn't know. He doesn't know her eye color, doesn't know her favorite food, or favorite color. He can't tell you how old she is or where she grew up. You ask him if he even has met this girl or if he just ordered her from a catalog. He responds that he knows her really well and that he doesn't have to know anything about her because he knows her as a person, he knows her heart. What do you think of your friend?

I'd say that you can't really know someone without knowing something about them. It's not like there is a checklist of 101 things that you have to find out about a person before you can get married, but in spending time with a person, you just naturally will learn things about them. It is the same thing with God. You don't need to set out to memorize a bunch of Bible trivia, but as you spend time with Him, you should just naturally learn some things about Him and His Word.

One of my favorite Bible verses is Romans 12:2, which says: "*Don't be conformed any longer to the pattern of this world, but be transformed by the renewing of your mind.*"(NIV) One of the submarines most helpful in the process of renewing our mind is studying. Our mind is renewed while thinking (studying) about things that will make it rejuvenated. Philippians 4:8 gives us a road map of where we might begin our studies. It says: "*Finally, brothers, whatever is true, whatever is noble, whatever is right, whatever is pure, whatever is lovely, whatever is admirable — if anything is excellent or praiseworthy — think about such things.*" (NIV)

The Bible is all of these things and is our primary source for studying the things of God. But there are other things that we can study as well: nature, human interactions, anything that fits the description of Philippians 4:8. You might notice that the things I am suggesting you study are the same things I told you to meditate on. This is because meditation is a part of studying; it is one of the things that you need to do if you want to fully understand the passage.

Imagine you could have Shakespeare with you while you are studying Hamlet. You find a particularly difficult passage and you ask Shakespeare, 'What does this mean?" and he explains it to you himself. This is what meditating on a passage can do for us; it allows us to hear God explain to us what a passage means, or how it should apply to our life. Sometimes, however, Shakespeare may tell you "I don't want to ruin the story for you. It's in the text; keep studying. You'll figure it out." Sometimes God does the same thing for us.

2 Timothy 2:8 says *"Study to show yourself approved unto God, a workman that does not need to be ashamed, rightly dividing the word of truth."* (NKJV) God wants you to dig in for yourself and discover the truths that He has hidden in His Word for you.

In Matthew 13, Jesus had just told His disciples some parables and He asks them in verse 51: *"Have you understood all these things?"* They replied *"Yes,"* Then in verse 52, he tells them *"Therefore every teacher of the law who has been instructed about the kingdom of heaven is like the owner of a house who brings out of his storeroom new treasures as well as old."* (NIV)

The storeroom is your mind, and what Jesus is saying is that the disciples had indeed understood some of the treasures that were in the parable he told. Additionally, Jesus was asserting that if they came back and studied the parable later, they would be able to pull the old treasures out to teach to others, but they would also find new insights and ideas that they hadn't noticed before. No matter how much we learn about God and His word, there are always more things there for us to discover.

Many Christians remain in bondage to fear, anxiety, strongholds and addictions because they neglect the important work of studying God's word. John 8:32 says, *"You shall know the truth and the truth shall set you free."* We often hear only the end of that verse quoted – "...the truth shall set you free." But, according to the verse, it is not just the truth, but our knowledge of it that sets us free. Unfortunately, too many Christians only know the truths that were taught them by others. So, if their pastor failed to teach in a particular area, or worse yet, taught some false doctrine, then they are often left in bondage in that area.

So how do we actually go about studying the Bible for ourselves? What are the actual steps to searching for treasure in God's Word? Firstly, there are some great Bible study guides out there that can help get you started on your journey. Each lesson usually covers a topic and guides you in learning what the Bible has to say on that subject. These guides are like baby food. They are one step up from the milk you get just coming and listening to someone else. You can put it in your own mouth, but it is already cut up into manageable pieces for you. Some of them are more advanced than others, maybe they aren't baby food, but more like TV dinners. If this is where you are on your spiritual journey, that's great. At least you are starting to feed yourself. Maybe you have been existing on milk up until now and you would like to start with these prepared guides. There are many sites on the internet where you can go and download free Bible study guides. One of my personal favorites is www.bibleschools.com.

God really wants you to grow to the point where not only are you feeding yourself, but you are doing your own cooking, too! Maybe not all the time; we all are busy and sometimes all we have time for is a TV dinner, but at least part of the time. So how do you go about doing spiritual cooking? What are the ingredients that go into a good Bible study?

The first ingredient is repetition. You should spend some time each day just doing some Bible reading. But that isn't the same thing as Bible study. Bible study involves looking more deeply into a passage. Begin by reading the passage at least two or three times. I recommend reading out loud because it helps you to concentrate. Otherwise, if you're like me you can get to the end of the chapter and find that you don't have a clue what you just read. So read the passage out loud and repeat it several times. Psychologists have discovered that repeating something over and over again ingrains that thought pattern in our mind. What they have found is that you don't even have to believe what you are repeating. Just the act of repeating it changes your thought patterns and behaviors. That's why self-help books tell you to repeat things like "*I am a strong, intelligent, woman*" over and over. Of course, if you're a man, this may cause you some gender identification issues.

The second ingredient is concentration. We are used to thinking about 10 different things at once and we constantly have a running list in our head of all the things that we have to do. This ingredient asks us to put all those thoughts aside and to give ourselves fully to the task of hearing God's Word speak to us. Meditation is one the things we could use at this point to help us accomplish our goal. Simply praying before you begin and asking God to help you focus your mind is another important way to concentrate. As I mentioned before, reading out loud can help. Keep a pen and paper handy to write down any insights or questions you have. And that leads us to the third ingredient, which is curiosity.

You need to ask a lot of questions. There are two categories of questions you should ask: Questions about the text and questions of the text. Questions about the text include questions like: *"Who was this passage addressed to? Why was this passage written? What is the main point of this passage? How does this passage fit with other parts of the Bible? What are the key words or phrases from this passage?"* In order to help you answer these questions, you will need a good study Bible with cross-references, a concordance, several different versions of the Bible and maybe a Bible commentary.

The first thing you will do is read the passage in several different versions. Be sure to note any differences you see. The next thing you will do is to look at the chapters before and after the one you are reading to try and give yourself some more of the context of what you are studying. Then you can check the cross-references, which are the texts usually listed in the center margin of your study Bible. They take you to other passages that deal with issues similar to the passage you are studying.

Next, use a concordance to look up the words you determined were the key words from the passage. If you still have some unanswered questions at this point, you may want to check a good Bible commentary, which can often give you more insight into the culture and background of the people to whom the passage was originally addressed.

If all of this sounds hard and time-consuming, that's because it is. Fortunately, it isn't necessary for you to do all of this in order to still gain a great benefit from Bible study. I told you there are two sets of question you must ask. The second set of questions are the ones you ask of the text. They include things like: "What is this text teaching me about God? What is God saying to me through this text? What is God telling me I need to change in my life through this text?"

These questions don't require a concordance, or a commentary; they require a listening ear and an open heart. If you answered the first set of questions, you can often get more insight to help you with the second. However, even if you skip the questions about the text, you can still answer these questions and get a real benefit for your life. Unfortunately, many Christians reverse this. They spend time digging deep and finding out all about the text, but then they neglect to apply it to their life. There are a whole bunch of people who can tell you how many clean and unclean animals Noah took on the ark, but they have no idea what God wants them to do today.

The final ingredient is insight. Many times, I have the experience of reading a passage I have studied dozens of times and discovering something I never noticed before. This is what Jesus was talking about when He said that we would draw out of our storehouses new treasures.

I wish I could give you a magic formula for getting insight, but there isn't one. Wisdom and insight come from God. All we can do is ask Him for it and then wait by faith for Him to show us what He wants to teach us. When we ask Him for wisdom in interpreting a passage, however, we can be confident that He will give it. Our part is to stay in the text and wait for it. James 1:5 says: *"If any of you lacks wisdom, he should ask God, who gives generously to all without finding fault, and it will be given to him."* (NIV)

# 5
# Fasting – Feasting in the Spirit

The submarine I want to examine in this chapter is one that is very underused in Christian churches today — fasting. Fasting has gone out of style in our day and age. We live in a culture that says do whatever makes you feel good. So why would you ever want to voluntarily go without food?

Well, have you ever been so engrossed in a project that you simply forgot to eat a meal? Suddenly it's dinner time and you're starving and you realize that you never stopped for lunch. It happens to me all the time. God wants you to be so engrossed in Him that you forget to eat.

But that is not the only reason to fast. Fasting can bring us great spiritual breakthroughs. Elmer Towns in his book "Fasting for Spiritual Breakthrough" lists nine biblical fasts. If you want to learn more about fasting, I recommend this book as a great place to start.

In this chapter, we are going to look briefly at those nine biblical examples, plus one more to make it a round number for my OCD readers. Each example gives us a different perspective on how we can use fasting to bring us closer to God.

I want to start off by saying that prayer must always accompany fasting. The whole point is to give up the time that you would normally use meeting your physical needs and instead devote it to your spiritual needs. It is a way of recognizing that your spiritual needs are greater than your physical needs. I like to think of my fasting days as spiritual feast days because I take the time I would normally use for preparing, eating and cleaning up my meals and devote it to prayer and Bible study. Prayer is really the key. If fasting isn't accompanied by prayer, you're not really fasting; you're just hungry.

In Mark 9, there is a story of a demon-possessed boy who was brought to Jesus' disciples, but they couldn't cast the demons out. After Jesus cast out the demon, the disciples wanted to know why they couldn't do it. Jesus told them "*This kind comes out only by prayer and fasting.*" It wasn't that the disciples didn't have the authority. The problem was they were trying to prove which one them was the greatest. They were harboring sin in their lives. They needed to fast and pray so that they could be freed from their own sin first. From this story, we can see that one of the purposes for fasting is to free us from addictions, sin and demonic activity in our life and the life of others.

Ezra 8 tells us that the Jews were returning from captivity and God had used Ezra to ask for and receive from the king all the articles that had been stolen from the temple as well as supplies to rebuild it with. I got out my calculator to figure out the value of just the gold that they brought back. The Bible says they had 100 hundred talents. This is equivalent to 3.75 tons in today's measurements. With gold prices at over $1,200 ounce, that is over $100,000,000 in gold that they were carrying. Basically, the whole treasury of Judah had been raided when Babylon took over, but now it was being generously returned.

But Ezra had been bragging to the king about how great God is so he was embarrassed to then ask the king for soldiers to protect them while they transported this stuff hundreds of miles by ox cart. So, he calls a fast and everyone fasts and asks God to protect them from thieves and attacks. God does and it all arrives safely in Jerusalem. From this story, we learn that one of the reasons we can fast is to ask God to watch over our finances.

This is especially true if it is for His glory and honor. And it will be if we really live our lives by Matthew 6:33, which says to seek first the kingdom of God and His glory and all these things (financial resources) will be added unto you. If we live our lives this way and people know it, then it is for God's glory to protect our finances. What fasting does is help reveal to us whether our motives are really for God's glory or our greed. It also demonstrates to the universe that we are serious about seeking God ahead of our own needs, including food.

1 Samuel 7 tells us the story of the Israelites seeking God after the Ark of the Covenant — the symbol of God's presence, which had been stolen by the Philistines — was returned. Israel decided to get rid of their idols and seek God. They were fasting for spiritual revival. Now it's true that they were also seeking protection from their enemies, but verse 2 says that they *"mourned and sought after the Lord."* This was a time of earnest seeking for a deeper walk with God. This was primarily a fast for the power of God to be manifest in their lives. This is precisely the kind of fast that I believe is most urgently needed today.

1 Kings 19 tells the story of Elijah right after he had successfully called down fire from heaven in the sight of all Israel, proving that God was the true God, not Baal. But then he hears the queen wants to kill him and he runs for His life. He ends up being alone and depressed. He goes straight from this mountain top experience into the depths of despair. Somehow, this seems to

happen to us a lot in our life. We go from this great experience with God and then we forget all about it when trouble comes and we get discouraged. Verses 3 and 4 say Elijah was afraid and ran for his life. When he came to Beersheba in Judah, he left his servant there, while he himself went a day's journey into the desert. He came to a broom tree, sat down under it and prayed that he might die.

How often we are like Elijah. We go from this great high and then our emotions crash and we just want to die. An angel gives Elijah something to eat, and on the strength of that meal, he fasts for 40 days as he journeys to the mountain of God. At the end of that time, he finally hears from God and God is able to shake him out of his depression and fear. This story illustrates that fasting can help us to get free from depression and anxiety; it can help us to hear the voice of God.

What happens when we are depressed is that our perspective is off; we can't see past our problems. The problems seem like they are going to crush us and we can't see our way out. What fasting does is help us to change our perspective; it can help us to hear God's voice and realize that our problems aren't too big for God to handle. We have the most powerful being in the universe on our side, so what do we have to fear?

1 Kings 17 tells the story of the widow of Zarapheth whom God sent Elijah to visit during the famine of that time. Elijah asked her to make him a cake to eat. She does, even though doing so requires the last of the food that she has. She had planned on eating a last meal with her son and then starving to death. Instead, she listens to Elijah and gives him the last of her food. She chooses to fast to help him. God worked a miracle and she ended up having enough to eat for the rest of the famine.

This teaches us that one of the reasons we can fast is to help others. In fact, when early Christians fasted, they used to give the food, or the monetary equivalent of what they would have eaten, to the poor. That is the idea with the 30-hour famine that people often do to raise money to help those who are starving around the world. Not only does this help others, but at the same time, it helps us to identify with the suffering that they are going through; it helps us to empathize with those who are truly poor in our world. Of course, the story shows that there is also a benefit to us when we do this. The widow was blessed much more for her act than Elijah was. In the same way, when we fast to help other people, we will also receive a blessing for ourselves.

Acts 9:9 tells us that Paul fasted while he was waiting for God to tell Him what to do. Sometimes we don't know what God wants us to do; we are confused and unsure. We can fast to ask God to give us direction. Sometimes when we pray, we tend to get tired and drift off; our thoughts are unfocused. Fasting actually helps clear our mind so that when we pray and listen for God's voice, our mind is more alert and able to hear God's whispers.

Daniel 1:3-14 tells the story of Daniel and his three friends when they first came to Babylon. They didn't do a total fast, but instead, they chose to eat only fruits and vegetables. They were asking God for health, because after 10 days, they were going to be compared to every other captive. If they didn't look as healthy, they would be forced to eat food that had been offered to idols. After 10 days, they were found to be healthier than everyone else. This is just one of the examples we have in scripture of people fasting and praying for health or healing. God didn't always answer those requests with healing; sometimes He did, but sometimes God says no. Health and healing, nevertheless, are legitimate reasons for us to fast.

*Fasting – Feasting in the Spirit*

John 1:3-4 tells us about John the Baptist who engaged in a specific kind of fasting. He ate only locusts and honey. He didn't want to waste his time thinking about food. He ate whatever was handy in the wilderness where he lived, which was locusts and honey. He was very focused on his mission. You could say he was fasting for more spiritual influence. Jesus says that among those born of woman, there is none greater than John, so he was pretty successful in that. One of the things that we can fast for is for greater influence. Many people are familiar with the prayer of Jabez, asking God to enlarge his territory. We can pray this prayer, and if we combine it with fasting, it will have even more power in our lives.

Esther 4:15-16 takes place in the context of a familiar story. The Jews are being persecuted and are slated for annihilation. The king doesn't know that Esther the queen is a Jew. She has to go before him and plead for the lives of her people. The problem is that appearing before the king without an invitation is a capital offense. Esther fasts and asks everyone to fast with her as she prepares to face the king. This story teaches us that one of the reasons we can fast is to help us face danger.

In Daniel 10:3, Daniel is fasting because he had received a vision and he didn't know what it meant. He was fasting for spiritual understanding. This is one of the best reasons to fast and one of the coolest stories in the Bible. The angel shows up and tells Daniel that he left heaven with Daniel's answer as soon as he asked, but it took him three weeks to fight his way there. I don't know what part Daniel's fasting for those three weeks had in that spiritual warfare, but I am sure they were connected.

Fasting is probably a fairly new idea for most of you, so I want to spend a few minutes just talking about some of the practical parts of fasting. One of the easiest ways to get started fasting is with a 24-hour fast. What you will do is eat dinner like you normally would, but the next morning you don't have breakfast (which actually means "break the fast") and you skip lunch. Then you have dinner as usual. So, you really are only missing two meals. After you have done a few 24-hour fasts, then you might want to try a 36-hour fast where you don't eat all three meals in a day.

The temptation people have when they are going to try fasting is to eat a really huge meal to try to get you through and then to break the fast with another huge meal. What you really want to do however is to eat a very light meal to begin and end your fast. This makes it a lot easier on your digestive tract. Avoid fatty foods and foods that are high in protein as these are hard for your body to get rid of while you are fasting.

Some of you might have diabetes or other medical reasons why you can't fast. For some people, doing a juice fast is a good option. This is when you don't eat solid food, but you drink fruit juices to help keep your blood sugar up. For some people, even that isn't possible. I would recommend that you try a different type of fasting. For example, you might decide to do a media fast where you turn off your TV, your radio, your iPod, your computer, etc. You fast from all forms of media or electronics and you take the time you would normally use doing those things and you devote them to God. This can be a great form of fasting even for those who *are* able to do food fasts. In fact, I find combining the two types of fasts to be especially effective.

I realize that fasting isn't something most people have really given any serious consideration to, let alone tried. I want to encourage you to give it a try. Start small, but really put your heart into and use this tool to sincerely seek God. I know that you won't be disappointed because God promises we will find Him if we seek Him with all of our heart. I hope that fasting will help you to engage your whole heart in that endeavor.

# 6

# Confession: Not just for Catholics

There is an old story that a pastor, a priest, and a rabbi went out fishing together. They got to talking and started bemoaning the fact that they each had sin in their life, but they didn't feel like there was anyone they could talk to about it because of their leadership positions. The rabbi suggested that since they were all alone in the middle of the lake, they could confess to each other and help each other with their problems. The others agreed, and the priest volunteered to go first. He admitted that he was an alcoholic and was often sneaking into the wine for communion. He even admitted being a little drunk on occasion when he was performing mass. The other two men nodded their heads and promised to pray for him.

The rabbi decided to go next. He admitted he had cheated on his wife several years before, and that he was still struggling with lustful thoughts. Apparently, there was a child that had resulted from the affair. No one knew that the boy was his son even though he and his mother still attended the rabbi's synagogue each week. The other two were totally shocked at this admission, but they managed to hide their shock and promised to pray for him. Finally, it was the pastor's turn. He said, "I have a terrible problem with gossip and I can't wait to get back to shore!"

This story illustrates one of the reasons this topic can be so scary for a lot of people. It is a scary thing to open up and share your dirt with another person. But doing so has the potential of bringing real healing to our lives.

When they hear the word confession, most people think of a priest in a little confessional box, with people going in and saying, "Forgive me, Father, for I have sinned." The priest then decides how bad the sin was and assigns some kind of penance to be performed. Usually, repeating certain prayers over and over again.

This isn't the Biblical form of confession. 1 John 1:9 says *"If we confess our sins, He is faithful and just to forgive us our sins and to cleanse us from all unrighteousness."* (KJV) We don't have to do penance when we confess our sin. As soon as we confess our sin to God, he forgives us.

It might seem that other people aren't involved at all! However, James 5:16 says to confess our sins to one another. That is one text most of would prefer to overlook, and for the most part, we do. There is something terrifying in the thought of talking to other people about our sins. The first question people ask is, "Why is this necessary?" The Bible makes it clear that because of Christ's sacrifice, we can confess our sins directly to God. Besides this, Jesus is our high priest so we are assured of forgiveness.

Why, then, would we confess our sins to another person? 1 Peter 2:9 gives us a clue. It says that we are all priests. A priest is a mediator between God and man. We no longer need a mediator between God and man since Jesus tore down the veil. On the other hand, the Bible says that we are all priests and have the honor of acting as a mediator between God and other people. In John 20:23 Jesus is talking to his disciples after the resurrection and he says: *"If you forgive the sins of any, they are forgiven them; if you retain the sins of any, they are retained."* (NKJV) There appears to be a contradiction here. How do we reconcile the fact that the Bible says we can confess our sin directly to God, and he will always forgive us, with the texts that say we are priests and if we don't forgive people their sin remains.

The way I have come to understand it is that when we confess our sins to God, He forgives us. However, the physical, emotional, and psychological consequences of our sin remain. Many times, even though God has forgiven us, we can't forgive ourselves. When we confess our sin to another person and they speak God's forgiveness to us, we start to learn to forgive ourselves and the healing process begins. In fact, that is what James 5:16 is trying to tell us. It says to confess our sins to each other so that we can be healed.

On the other hand, if someone confesses their sin and you refuse to offer them forgiveness, the Bible says the sin is retained. Now, why would you refuse to offer someone forgiveness? I can only think of two possible reasons. Either they have sinned against you personally and you don't want to forgive them, or they have done something similar to the action of someone else who you don't want to forgive. This is very dangerous ground since Matthew 6:15 tells us that God won't forgive us if we don't forgive other people.

It is very important for you to realize what happens when someone sins against you. When someone does something to you, your souls are bound together and both of you reap the consequences of their sin. It isn't fair, but it is the nature of sin. That is one of the reasons why God hates sin. If someone stabs you with a knife, it isn't fair that you are the one who is in pain and has to heal from your wounds, but that is the way it is. Such an attack wouldn't just wound our body, but also our spirit. Healing for our body will come naturally, but our spirit can't begin to heal until we have forgiven the person.

We think forgiveness is for the other person, but in reality, forgiveness is for us. God gave it to us as way of releasing ourselves from the bondage we were put in by someone else's sin. When we speak forgiveness to someone, it allows both them and us to begin to heal. Even our physical health and healing is affected by unforgiveness in our life. Even the medical community is beginning to recognize this fact.

I have shared with you why forgiveness is so important, but you may still be wondering why John 20:23 says that if we don't forgive someone's sin, the sin is retained. Let's pretend I did something to someone 20 years ago. I confessed that sin to God and I asked the person to forgive me, but they refused. Is God going to keep me out of heaven because they wouldn't forgive me? I chose to quote this text from the New King James Version because I think in this instance it most accurately captures the idea of the original text, and some of the other translations are even more problematic.

The text says that the sin is retained. I don't believe that it can mean that God won't forgive it, because God has promised to forgive any sin we confess to him. Instead, I believe this means that the results of the sin will be alive in both the person who committed the sin and the person harmed by the sin who refused to forgive him. The text doesn't say where the sin is retained. I believe it is at least partly retained by the person who won't forgive.

It reminds me of a story I heard one time about an old codger who hated his next door neighbor. They had been feuding for years when God decided to teach the man a lesson. He sent an angel to him to tell him that God would do for him whatever he asked. He could ask for a billion dollars, great health, long life, happiness — anything at all. The only stipulation was, whatever he asked for, his neighbor would receive twice as much. The old man growled, "Then I want God to strike me blind in one eye." This is essentially what we are doing when we refuse to forgive someone who has wronged us.

Sometimes people carry this anger with them so long they don't even realize they are doing it. If you are a person who suffers from depression or other emotional problems, there are a lot of different things that could be causing it. One of the things to ask yourself though is: Are there people who have hurt me that I have never forgiven? If your answer is yes, this could be contributing to your problem.

There is a lot more I could say about forgiveness, but this submarine isn't about forgiveness. It's about confession. It is obvious to us that we need to confess our sin to someone when they are the person we have wronged. What is less obvious is that we also need to confess our sin to someone else when our sin is between God and us. We need to do this because confessing to another person allows them to speak forgiveness into our life that allows healing to take place in our life.

Naturally, we have to be careful about who we choose to confess to and how we do it. We don't want to end up confessing to someone like the pastor who was in the boat with the Rabbi and the priest! I am going to describe to you the best way to go about receiving confession from others. This will make it clear to you what you should look for in someone else when you feel the need to confess.

If someone is going to confess to us, we need be able to hear anything without being horrified. You can't fake this. If someone tells you about some heinous act and you are horrified by it, you won't be able to hide it. It will be written all over your face. How do you get there? Do you watch all kind of movies filled with every kind of filth imaginable so that you become desensitized and nothing bothers you? No, paradoxically you do this by being horrified by all sin. Once we have been truly horrified by the dreadfulness of our own sin that nailed Jesus to the cross, then we will no longer be horrified by even the dirtiest sin of someone else.

When you live in this reality, people sense that you are safe to talk to, that you will never betray their trust. People tell me things all the time and they are often surprised that I'm not shocked by what they are telling me. When they express this, I am tempted to tell them, "Are you kidding? You should hear what Bobby did." I don't do that for two very important reasons. First, when you are receiving confession from someone, you must never share what you hear with someone else. Secondly, although it is tempting to break the tension with an off-handed comment, it is very important that you don't lighten what should be a heavy moment.

Instead, just inwardly pray for the person while you listen. Don't tell them that their sin is no big deal. Even if it is a small thing that you don't consider a sin, if it is coming between them and God then it is a very big deal. Resist the urge to excuse their sin. Instead, listen fully to the person. Then, place your hands on them and pray for them. Then announce that the forgiveness of Jesus is real and effective in their life.

When you have something on your heart that you want to confess to a fellow Christian, you should look for someone you believe can do all the things we just talked about. When you decide to confess your sins, there are three things that you need to do.

First of all, you must examine your conscience in order to discover what things God wants to remove from your life. There are different ways that you can do this. One way is to meditate and ask the Holy Spirit to bring to your mind anything that isn't right in your life. Another way is to go through the Ten Commandments and measure yourself against them. For example, the first commandment says: "*You shall have no other Gods before me.*" So, you might spend a few minutes asking yourself if there is anything in your life that has become too important and is taking the place of God in your life. What is crowding out your time with God?

The second step of confession is to have a real sorrow for sin. I am not talking about an emotion; you don't have to cry and moan. Sorrow for sin means that we realize how much it cost Jesus. It means we know in our innermost being that our sin killed Him. We realize the seriousness of what we have done. Then confession isn't just some lip service we are giving, but we truly understand the magnitude of sin in our life and it horrifies us. This isn't something that we can work up in ourselves; we have to ask God to do it. This step involves asking God to show you the way that he views your sin and what it cost him. Invite God to give you a Godly sorrow for what you have done.

Finally, we must have a determination to avoid sin. We can't have the attitude that says, "*Oh well. God will forgive me so I'll just ask for forgiveness and go back out and sin again*." You can't be planning your next sin while you are confessing your last one. Repentance means a turning away from sin. That doesn't mean that you won't ever sin again or even that you won't commit the same sin over and over again. It just means that each time you confess, your heart must be truly set on getting rid of the sin and allowing Jesus to live His perfect life in us.

# 7
# The Fellowship of the Trinity

The submarine I want to bring to your attention in this chapter is the submarine of fellowship. We use the word fellowship kind of lightly. We have fellowship dinner in the fellowship hall, and there are fellowship socials. If you put the word fellowship in front of something, it makes it sound more holy. Now you are finding out that fellowship is a submarine; perhaps you are getting excited. Finally, a submarine you can really enjoy. Maybe you are thinking, "We can have a fellowship ice cream social and it will bring me closer to Jesus? Hallelujah!"

I hate to disappoint anyone, but having fun together is a part of fellowship, but it isn't the main part. The way the word fellowship is used today has been reduced to getting together to have fun, but that isn't the primary definition. We read in Acts 2:42 that one of the four things that the new converts devoted themselves to was fellowship. They didn't devote themselves to it because it was fun. They devoted themselves to it because it was one of the things that could help them to grow.

The real meaning of fellowship is probably best illustrated by the fellowship of the ring from the popular book and movie series "The Lord of the Rings." The fellowship was formed for the purpose of destroying the ring. The ring was a lot like sin. It appeared to give power and control to the person who used it, but it actually took control over that person. It was very hard to get rid of, and would ultimately be impossible for anyone to do it alone.

The fellowship was buried under an avalanche on top of a mountain; attacked by a sea monster; they got lost deep in a cave where they were chased by trolls and other fearsome creatures; and they had to battle thousands of orcs. Now there is a group that enjoyed some great fellowship!

True fellowship happens when a group of people are pursuing a shared goal, and in the process, they go through some shared experiences. Those experiences may be positive or negative, but it is the sharing of the experiences that creates community. However, the worse the circumstances are, the stronger the bond will be. That is why soldiers who have been through battle together are often friends for life. The fellowship they enjoy is birthed in hardship, so it lasts a long time.

To be Christian fellowship, however, our fellowship must include Christ in the circle. We aren't just sharing experiences with other people; we are sharing our experiences with Jesus. 1 John 1:3 says, *"We proclaim to you what we have seen and heard, so that you also may have fellowship with us. And our fellowship is with the Father and with his Son, Jesus Christ."* (NIV) In other words, we don't just fellowship with each other, we all enter the fellowship of the trinity together. We don't create community; we enter into the community God created. Christian fellowship happens when a group of people experience the presence of God together.

1 Corinthians 1:9 says, *"God, who has called you into fellowship with his Son Jesus Christ our Lord, is faithful."* (NIV) God is calling us to be in fellowship with Jesus. Jesus gave up his ability to be in all places at once when He became human. That means that the only way most us will ever experience Jesus directly is through His body, which is His church. When I allow God to use me, and you allow God to use you, then when we get together, I get to be Jesus' hands and feet to minister to you, and you get to be His voice and eyes to minister to me. This can only happen when we all have the

Holy Spirit living in us. That is why 2 Corinthians 13:14 calls it the fellowship of the Holy Spirit.

Earlier I mentioned that the worse the circumstances are that a group of people go through, the stronger the bond will be. A few years ago, I remember watching the release of the miners who had been trapped in the mine down in Chile and the news commentator was interviewing an expert who said that all the miners would likely remain very close for life. They cited an example of a plane that had crashed in the mountains 40 years before. The survivors almost starved to death and even resorted to cannibalism. Forty years later, they all still get together on the anniversary of their rescue to celebrate. The expert said that the gathering actually got bigger each year because all of their extended family came too and the whole group is just like one big family.

Philippians 3:10 says "*I want to know Christ and the power of his resurrection and the fellowship of sharing in his sufferings, becoming like him in his death*". (NIV) The highest honor anyone could have ever had would have been to suffer with Christ. Imagine if you could be bonded together with Him in the same way that those miners are bonded together. Philippians is telling us that when we suffer as Christians and we share that suffering with our brothers and sisters in Christ, then we are sharing in the suffering of Jesus.

The real purpose of fellowship is to struggle together to hear God's voice and to encourage each other to wholeheartedly follow God. There is no one who could build a submarine that would be able to go very deep by themselves. It requires a huge team of people, resources, and factories to build a submarine. In this same way, if we want to go profoundly deep with God, we need others. When we experience going deep with God together, it bonds us together in a special way that nothing else can do.

Acts 4:31-33 describes such an event and the results that happened. It says: "*When they had prayed, the place where they were gathered together was shaken; and they were all filled with the Holy Spirit and spoke the word of God with boldness. Now the company of those who believed were of one heart and soul, and no one said that any of the things which he possessed was his own, but they had everything in common. And with great power the apostles gave their testimony to the resurrection of the Lord Jesus, and great grace was upon them all.*"(NIV)

Just before this happened, the apostles were arrested for preaching in Jesus' name. They were threatened and told to stop preaching. They had just gone through this shared experience of being persecuted. Then they prayed together. I don't believe this was a perfunctory prayer, I believe they were wrestling with God in prayer, pleading for more of His spirit. Look at the results; they were of one heart and soul. They shared everything; it became a true communist utopia.

Modern day communism tried to imitate this and it has resulted in disaster. Why? They are trying to force this system on people who aren't of one heart and soul. Sharing things with other people must come from a heart filled with love. You can't force that on someone else. Love that is forced isn't love at all; it's rape.

Fellowship is the process by which we develop a deeper love for each other. 1 John 2:9-10 says *"Anyone who claims to be in the light but hates his brother is still in the darkness. Whoever loves his brother lives in the light, and there is nothing in him to make him stumble."* (NIV) To put it another way, you can't have a deep love for God without also having a deep love for His people.

Learning to love others is essential to your spiritual growth. God has always existed in community. In Genesis 1:26, God says:

"*Let **us** make man in our image...*" (NIV, emphasis supplied). God didn't say, "*I will make man in my image.*" He said, "*Let us make man in our image.*" God exists in community.

All through the first chapter of Genesis, it describes God creating things followed by the phrase "and God saw that it was good." Then he creates man and in Genesis 2:18 He says, "*It is not good that man should be alone.*" This is the first time that something isn't good. God knew that for a man to be in His image, he had to be in community.

We need other people in our life. In fact, a study done in Alameda County, California a few years ago found that people who were isolated were three times as likely to die than the most relationally connected people. Amazingly, they found that people who had bad habits like smoking but lots of friends, would outlive people who had no bad habits but no close relationships either. Being in a small group could save your life!

A few years ago, a small plane crashed into the Pacific Ocean carrying eight people. One of the people on board was a pastor named Neil Watts. He couldn't bear the thought that they all might die that night and he didn't know if the other passengers had a relationship with Jesus or not. He tried to convince everyone to stay together so that he would have the chance to share his faith with them in case they didn't make it.

Two people didn't listen to him and decided to go off on their own. One other man stayed with them for a while, but then drifted off on his own. He and the other two were never heard from again. The five who remained together, however, prayed and encouraged each other. They swam for six hours before they finally reached the shore. None were strong swimmers, but by the grace of God they made it.

Pastor Watts later attempted to swim for six hours on his own just to see if he could do it. He didn't even last half an hour. It was only the power of God and the fellowship of others that got them through this terrible ordeal.

So how do we get there? What are the practical things that we do to help us enter into the fellowship God wants us to have? First of all, in order to enter into Christian fellowship, you must spend time with other believers. You can't really love someone that you don't know. So, the first step is getting together with other Christians outside of church. Join a small group, find a prayer partner, call up another member and ask them to go to a movie with you.

The second step is the scary step. To really know and be known, we must be vulnerable with other people. We must share things with people that we would rather keep secret. Tell people about your failures and the pain that you have experienced in your life. If you want to experience healing in your life, tell other people about it and allow them to share in your suffering.

Thirdly, we must spend time in prayer and in worship together seeking God. Worshipping God in a large group at church is fine. But, there are many distractions. People come in and out and not everyone is really keyed into worshiping God. Maybe the band is too loud for you, or you don't like the songs.

In a small group, a lot of those factors are mitigated. There is something profound that happens when a small group of people comes together to seek God with all their hearts. When everyone present is really worshipping God with their whole hearts I've discovered that God reveals Himself in a powerful way. If you want to know what I am talking about, try spending at least half the night praying and worshipping with a small group of believers.

Finally, we must make ourselves available to God as a group to be used for his purposes. When we do this, God will take us through experiences that will not only be a witness to the world but will bond us together because of the shared experience.

# 8

# Prayer: Spiritual Air

We have been talking about going into the depths with God — how to get below the waves and enjoy the peace and serenity of being in the presence of God. But there is one thing that shouldn't be overlooked. We are, in fact, creatures of the earth. We cannot exist in the depths without oxygen. Today we are going to look at a discipline that must accompany every submarine and is itself a submarine.

All true submarines must have an oxygen supply. Those that don't are merely submersibles and can't stay down very long. Most modern submarines can make oxygen through the electrolysis of water. Prayer is our spiritual oxygen. Without it, we cannot hope to survive in the deep things of God. It is only by this vital connection to God Himself that we can operate in the spiritual realm.

For the Christian, prayer must be as constant as breathing. Your spiritual life cannot survive any longer without prayer than your physical body can without oxygen. That is why 1 Thessalonians 5:17 tells us to pray without ceasing. But if that really is to be the norm for most Christians, then I am afraid that we have a lot of abnormal Christians. Unfortunately, I believe that really is the case.

The church is full of weak anemic Christians who could barely pray for half an hour let alone without ceasing. They come to church each week to get enough spiritual CPR to keep them going for another week, but they never experience the full power of God. They are missing out on the grand adventure God has planned for them.

I am not telling you this so you can beat yourself up about it. I know that you are reading this because you have a hunger for a deeper experience with God. You desire to walk with Him like Enoch did, but you just don't know where to start. You look around and nobody else seems to know either; everyone seems to be in the same boat. It is easy to assume that is just normal, that nobody really experiences a deep abiding relationship with God in which communication is constant and ongoing. That only a few super-saints like Moses and Elijah enjoyed that kind of relationship.

We can rest satisfied that we are saved by Christ's sacrifice and just shrug our shoulders and give up on having a Spirit-filled life now.

But while apathy and powerlessness in the church is very ordinary and commonplace, it is not normal. The normal Christian life — the life God intends for His people — is a life that is just like

Jesus. Galatians 2:20 says: "*I have been crucified with Christ and I no longer live, but Christ lives in me.*" (NIV) If you are dead and Christ lives in you, then you are going to be just like Jesus.

Jesus began His ministry by spending 40 days in the wilderness fasting and praying. There are several times in the gospels where Jesus spent the whole night in prayer. So, if Jesus is living in us, spending large amounts of time praying shouldn't be hard.

The problem is our old self keeps coming back to life. When we allow our old self to be in control, we call that walking in the flesh. When we allow Jesus to be in control, we call that walking in the Spirit. We have two natures warring against each other. Which one will win? The one that we feed! We feed the flesh by thinking sinful thoughts, and we feed the Spirit by prayer and the other submarines. If we are going to stay in the Spirit, we have to be in continual prayer.

Which brings us back full circle to our original problem. How can we possibly pray without ceasing when we get worn out after trying for 20 minutes? Besides, we have jobs and responsibilities to take care of; how could we possible pray all the time, even if we knew how to pray without getting fatigued?

I enjoy reading biographies of some of the great spiritual leaders of the past. Two of my favorite quotes on prayer come from Martin Luther and C.S. Lewis. Luther, when most pressed with work, is reported to have said, "*I have so much to do that I cannot get on without three hours a day praying.*" Most of us are just the opposite we think "*I have too much to do today. I can't take time out to pray.*" Luther realized that what He could do in His own power was worthless, so if he had a lot to do, he needed to spend extra time connecting to God so that he could have God's power to accomplish what He needed to do.

C.S. Lewis said: "*The moment you wake up each morning, all your wishes and hopes for the day rush at you like wild animals. And the first job each morning consists in shoving it all back; in listening to that other voice, taking that other point of view, letting that other, larger, stronger, quieter life come flowing in.*"[ii] These quotes inspire me to pray, and make prayer the first and most important part of my day.

I also read about Dwight Moody, John Hyde and Charles Spurgeon and how they were men of prayer. Many times, they would spend the whole night on their knees praying to God before they were to preach somewhere. After I had read one of these books, I would get inspired for a while and decide I was going to work up to praying all night like they did. Inevitably, I would fall short, get discouraged, and give up.

Finally, I realized I was striving for the wrong thing. These men didn't set out to pray all night, they prayed all night because they were in communion with the King of Kings and Lords of Lords and they didn't want to stop.

Your goal can't be to be a great prayer warrior or to show God how great you are by the time you are devoting to Him. Your goal simply should be to connect with the heart of God. When you do this, you won't want to leave His presence.

If you set out to spend a night in prayer, you might be able to grit your teeth and make it through, but won't really have accomplished anything unless you truly connect in an intimate way with the heart of God. Great prayers can't be measured merely by the time spent doing them, but by the heart connection to God that results.

I want to give you some practical steps to take to learn to pray great prayers — a training program for prayer warriors. I once preached a message called "How to pray for an hour without falling asleep." I realize now that I was giving people the wrong goal; your goal shouldn't be praying for an hour, it should be connecting to God. But the practical steps are going to be the same.

A spiritual workout isn't that different from a physical one. For example, if you decided that you wanted to be able to lift 500 pounds, you wouldn't go to the gym every day and try to lift 500 pounds, grunt and struggle and then leave the gym. That's not training, that's trying. You would go to the gym and put on the bar the amount of weight you can lift and you lift it as many times as you can. You come back the next day and try to do more. You keep doing that until you can lift 500 pounds.

In the same way, spiritually you don't start off by trying to spend the whole night in prayer. No, you start off praying as long as you are able and you try to pray a little more each day.

Now, a better goal than trying to lift 500 pounds would be to see your muscles get a little bigger each day. After all, the point of going to the gym isn't to learn how to lift weights; it is to change your body. In the same way, spiritually, your goal shouldn't be to pray for an hour, but to see your relationship with God grow a little stronger each day. The point of prayer isn't so you can get better at prayer, it is to get to know God.

There are four common problems that people have when they pray. The first problem is simply not knowing what to say. Part of the problem is that some people give the impression that when you talk to God, you must use special words, or you have to quote scripture. The truth is you can just talk to God from your heart. That is what He really wants. He wants to hear His children just talk with Him.

Having said that, it can be helpful to have a plan of what topics you might want to talk to Him about. If you were going to meet the Queen of England you might kind of plan out what you wanted to say to her in advance.

I've come up with an acronym that can help you remember four topics that I think are helpful to include in your conversations with God. You might want to divide your prayer time up into four sections so that you spend equal amounts of time on each topic. At first, it might seem a little rigid to use this, but after a while it becomes natural. Remember, everything is hard before it is easy.

*Prayer: Spiritual Air*

The acronym spells the word PATH, which is what the early church was called. They were known as followers of the path.

The P stands for Praise. We want to spend time praising God for who He is. God enjoys hearing His people praise Him. The A stands for Apologies, which is where we confess to God the things we have done wrong and we ask Him to reveal to us the things we still need to change. The T stands for Thanks. This is where we thank God for the things that He has done for us personally.

Sometimes people get confused because they don't know the difference between praise and thanks. If you think about it in relationship to yourself, the difference becomes clear. When someone praises you, they might say something like, "You are a great singer. You are a nice person. You are so good looking." When they thank you, they say things like, "Thanks for the loan. I really appreciate your help on my project. Thanks for watching my kids for me last night."

It is the same thing with God. When we are praising Him, we are extolling His character. When we are thanking Him, we are thanking Him for what He has done for us. They might overlap; sometimes you might not be sure what category something goes in. That's OK, the important thing is that you are doing both!

The H stands for Help. This is the one that most of us just naturally go to first. But save it for last instead. Make asking God for the things you need the last thing you do in prayer. That way you will already be in a conversation with God when you ask Him for what you need. Also, make sure you are praying for other people and their needs, not just your own.

The second problem that people often face in prayer is that their mind wanders off. How do you keep your mind focused when you pray?

I have three practical suggestions for you. One, have a set time and place for prayer. When you do this, you begin to associate that place with prayer so that as soon as you go there your mind begins automatically to enter into prayer. Having a regular time for prayer gets you into a rhythm that increases the ease with which we enter into prayer.

The second suggestion I have is to pray out loud. It really is a modern phenomenon to pray silently. God can read your thoughts and there is nothing wrong with praying silently, but praying out loud can help keep your mind focused. If you carefully study the

Bible, you will find that the norm for most Bible characters, including Jesus was to pray out loud.

One clear example is the story of Daniel. He prayed to God at his window (a set place) three times a day (a set time). Others heard Him; he prayed out loud. The king passed a law that said anyone who prayed to anyone other than the king for 30 days would be thrown into the lion's den. It would have been more expedient for Daniel to just pray silently, or maybe in a different place. But, it is clear Daniel continued to pray out loud at his window. (Others were able to hear him and prove he wasn't praying to the king.)

I heard a story recently about a man who took his small son with him to town one day to run some errands. When lunch time arrived, the two of them went to a familiar diner for a sandwich. The father sat down on one of the stools at the counter and lifted the boy up to the seat beside him. They ordered lunch, and when the waiter brought the food, the father said, *"Son, we'll just have a silent prayer."* Dad got through praying first and waited for the boy to finish his prayer, but he just sat with his head bowed for an unusually long time. When he finally looked up, his father asked him, *"What in the world were you praying about all that time?"* With the innocence and honesty of a child, he replied, *"How do I know? It was a silent prayer."*

The problem with silent prayer is that very often when we are done praying, our mind has wondered so much that we don't even know what we prayed about. There is nothing wrong with silent prayer if it works for you — if you don't have trouble with your mind wandering. However, if you have that problem, try praying out loud.

The third suggestion I have for overcoming the wandering mind is to find a posture that reminds you who you are talking to. You might try: kneeling, raising your hands, laying prostrate, or whatever position most helps you to focus your mind and remember who you are talking to.

The third problem people often face with prayer is falling asleep. I heard about a couple recently who were selling Christian books. One day the husband said to the wife, "*You are a better salesperson than I am. Why don't we work together? You do the presentation and I will pray.*" The next house they came to, the person invited them in, and the husband sat down on the couch to pray while the woman sat down at the table and began her presentation. She was just beginning the close when a loud snoring sound came from the couch.

It's a common problem we have; we are so busy that when we finally sit down our body goes, "*Ahh finally time to fall asleep.*" The only solution I have found is to follow the example of the patriarch Enoch who we are told walked with God. I personally have found that walking while praying keeps me alert and focused and able to focus on praying. If you can find a place in nature to walk, it is even better because God often speaks to us through creation. The bonus is if you are praying out loud, you don't have to worry about people thinking you're nuts.

The final problem I want to address is the problem of apathy. The surest fix is to have a prayer partner who is going to push you to pray and hold you accountable even when you don't feel like it. Early African converts to Christianity were earnest and regular in private devotions. Each one reportedly had a separate spot in the thicket where he would pour out his heart to God.

Over time, the paths to these places became well worn. As a result, if one of these believers began to neglect prayer, it was soon apparent to the others. They would kindly remind the negligent one, "Brother, the grass grows on your path." Do you have anyone who knows when the grass is growing on your path? I want to encourage you to find someone who will point out to you when you are slipping in your spiritual walk.

# 9
## Simple Simplicity

The kingdom of Heaven is like a Chinese bamboo tree. The soil is prepared and it is planted. For four years, all you will see is a tiny shoot on a small bulb. During this time, all of the growth happens beneath the surface where you can't see it. Then in the fifth year, the bamboo tree shoots up and can grow up to 80 feet in just the one year.

Sometimes people get discouraged because they look at their life and they don't see any changes. They say, *"These submarines might work for some people, but they're not working for me."* They get discouraged and give up. Those people somehow missed the point.

The submarines aren't meant to change your life; they are meant to help you connect to the heart of God. They are designed to take you into the depths of who He is. It is God who changes your life. Eventually, you will see explosive growth in your life just like the bamboo tree. It's not the submarines that do that, it is God. The submarines just help you get into His presence so He can do His work.

I have many times seen God do such incredible work in a person's life that everyone is just amazed that someone could change so dramatically and so fast. But the fact is, what we are seeing is really the result of years of work that God has been doing in their life that nobody could see. They might not have even known it themselves; they may have been just going about their life, but the Spirit was doing a work in them.

I am telling you this because the submarine I am describing today is both a submarine and a fruit of God's work in our life. Unlike many of the other submarines, it is an external reality that can be seen by others. I am talking about the submarine of simplicity. We live in a very complex world, and it is getting more complicated all the time.

My father-in-law has an entertainment center all set up with a satellite dish, a big screen television, a surround sound system, DVD Player, CD Player, AM/FM radio and MP3 player. He has like eight remotes for the things and it's hard to figure out what remote does what, and they are always getting lost. So, he bought a universal remote that controls all of them.

The only problem is, it is so complicated that he is the only one who can use it. If someone else wants to watch TV, listen to music, or change the channel, we have to go find him to do it for us. Sometimes the things that are supposed to make our life easier, make it more complicated and busy.

Science was supposed to make our lives easier and less complicated, but our world is getting more complex not less. If we are going to keep God's voice from being drowned out by the busyness, we are going to need to find ways to simplify and create some margins in our life.

There is a show on television called "Hoarders." I like watching it sometimes just to remind myself how silly it is to become attached to things in this world. The show tries to help people who are literally being buried alive in all their stuff. There are people on this show who literally have not been able to sleep in their bed or cook in their kitchen for years because they are buried in junk. Their family and friends won't come by to visit them because of the filth of their house.

Some of them are in danger of being forced to move because the health department is about to condemn their house because it is so unsanitary. The show sometimes must send people in wearing hazmat suits to get rid of the garbage that has piled up. But what amazes me is that the people will be angry and lash out because their precious stuff is being thrown away. What makes people hang on to garbage even when it is ruining their life?

Before you are too hard on them, I want you to think about the things in your own life that you are hanging on to that will appear as garbage in the light of eternity, but may be preventing you from having an abundant life now. It could be literal things, stylish clothes, a car, jewelry, or it might be pride, ambition, power, being well-liked or seeking a good time.

Ask yourself, "Am I too busy? Is my life too complicated?" If it is, you need to ask why. What are you striving for? Why are you driven to do what you do? It could even be good things like a desire to help people or to change the world. Whatever it is, if it is keeping you too busy to hear from God, you need to ruthlessly cut it from your life.

Imagine if a hoarder lived on a submarine. It would be terrible. Nobody would be able to do anything. It would ruin the function of the submarine. No, everything on a submarine must be simple. Every inch of a submarine is carefully thought out so that only the absolute necessities are left and they take up as little space as possible.

One of the reasons life is so complicated and busy is that we are taught that you must have things to be happy. We are taught not to wait for things, but to grasp them as soon as possible and buy them on credit if necessary. Appliances, computers, and cars are all designed to make our life simpler and easier. But any time that these devices save us is quickly gobbled up in the drive to get the next new thing that is coming out.

Many people can't park their cars in their garage because it is filled with all the things they bought last year, but hardly use. The fastest growing real estate market and the only segment that wasn't really affected by the recent housing bubble is storage units. Every year, Americans spend millions of dollars storing things that they may never use again. But the real cost of our obsession with things is broken families, broken relationships, and shallow spirituality.

Simplicity, at its heart, means getting rid of the values of the world — money, status, and power — and replacing them with God's values — truth, love, and holiness. Jesus said that we can't serve both God and money, so he advises us in Matthew 6:33 to "*Seek first the kingdom of heaven and His righteousness and all these things will be added unto you."*

Seeking first the kingdom of heaven means placing ourselves under God's authority. When we are under God's authority, we are a part of His heavenly kingdom. In other words, if we seek money and worldly possessions, those things will end up controlling us. But if we seek God, he will provide for our needs and we will be free from the worry and busyness that comes from seeking earthly goods.

Some of you are saying to yourselves, "Yeah, I know money is the root of all evil. But you're talking to the wrong person; I'm poor. I don't have money." What you are referring to is one of the most misquoted verses in the Bible. It comes from 1 Timothy 6:10 which says, *"For the love of money is the root of all evil: which while some coveted after, they have erred from the faith, and pierced themselves through with many sorrows."*(KJV) Money isn't the root of evil; the love of it is. It has been observed that those who have it least often love it most.

Being poor is no guarantee that you are living the simple life. The simple life is one that is totally and completely centered on the person of Jesus Christ. The focus of your energy and enthusiasm is consumed with pursuing God. You say, "Wait a minute. What do you mean, pursuing God? God pursues us, and when I became a Christian, I found Him." You are right about that, but the more you know God, the more you want to know Him.

I like the way A. W. Tozer puts it: "*To have found God and still to pursue Him is the soul's paradox of love, scorned indeed by the too-easily satisfied religionist, but justified in happy experience by the children of the burning heart.*"[iii]

God is the most valuable thing that you could ever have. I sometimes hear Christians obsessing about the fat cats on Wall Street or the obscene salaries of baseball players. I want to say, "Don't you realize how impoverished those people are without God?" Even if they are Christians, they must constantly fight the temptation to depend on their wealth rather than God. In Numbers 18:20, God told Aaron that his family would not receive an inheritance in Israel but that He Himself would be their inheritance. In other words, he made Aaron the wealthiest man who had ever lived. He said, "You don't need any earthly goods; I will take care of you."

When you come to realize that God really is all you need, then you are released from all anxiety and worry. If you see your job as the source of wealth, then you could lose that. That creates anxiety, but if God is the source of your wealth, you can never lose that. That is why Jesus said in Luke 6:20, "*Blessed are the poor for theirs is the kingdom of heaven.*" (NIV) In other words, like Aaron, those who are poor receive God Himself as their inheritance.

But in verse 24 he states, "*Woe to you who are rich for you have received your consolation.*" (NIV) Stated another way, those who are rich don't sense their need of God and so miss out on Him.

So, am I saying that we all need to quit our jobs and move into a monastery where we can spend all our time seeking God? No, seeking God must be our first thing, but not our only thing. Simplicity doesn't even mean that we won't be busy. We may be very busy, but all our busyness will have one purpose — God's purpose. We will not be distracted doing all kinds of things that have a thousand different motivations. Just as everything on a submarine has a purpose that contributes to the success of the ship, so everything we do will contribute to God's purpose in us. Everything we do must be done to the tempo of God's beating heart.

Simplicity is first and foremost a condition of the heart. It is cutting everything out of our heart that is not God. There are three attitudes that we must cultivate to achieve the simple life.

First, we must have an attitude of gratitude. 1 Timothy 6:8 says, *"Godliness with contentment is great gain."* (NIV) 1 Thessalonians 3:16 says, *"Give thanks in all circumstances for this is God's will for you in Christ Jesus."* (NIV) God wants you to praise Him no matter what circumstances you find yourself in. Doing this reveals your faith that He is, in fact, all you need and will take care of you.

The second attitude you need to cultivate is one that knows it is God's job to take care of what you have. People waste a lot of time and energy worrying about losing their possessions. If we can say, "Hey it's all God's. He can take care of it." that will release us from a lot of stress. That doesn't mean that you shouldn't lock your doors or buy insurance; God has placed you as steward over your possessions, but you shouldn't obsess about them. This principle applies not only to our physical possessions, but to our reputation, our health, our employment and every aspect of our life.

The third attitude to cultivate is one that says our possessions are available to others. If everything we have belongs to God — and it does belong to Him if God is the source of our wealth instead of our jobs — and we refuse to share with others when it is clearly right and good that we should, then we are really stealing those things from God.

Beside the internal attitudes, simplicity must also have an external aspect. Richard Foster in his book "Celebration of Discipline" gives 10 suggestions for bringing simplicity to our external world. But, before we look at those, a warning is in order. Few people will know how much time you spend in prayer, Bible study, meditation and many of the other submarines, but many people will be able to see how you are using this submarine. This creates a grave danger. It is easy to take things that God convicts us we need to do to simplify our life and make them rules for everyone else to follow. This leads to legalism that doesn't really simplify our life, but just becomes another checklist of things we do to try to please God.

The 10 suggestions Richard Foster gives are as follows.

- Buy things for their usefulness, not their status. Buy the Ford, not the Mercedes. Buy your clothes at Walmart or Target, not the mall or designer shops. Stop trying to impress people with your things and impress them with your life.

- Reject anything that is producing an addiction in you, no matter how innocent it seems. Whether it's music, chocolate, TV or whatever, cut it out of your life. Refuse to be a slave to anything except God. Now by definition, an addiction is something that is beyond your control. You can't just decide to be free of it. You must open this part of your life to God and ask Him to bring you healing and freedom
- Develop the habit of giving away things that mean a lot to you. Doing this breaks the hold that possessions have on you.
- Don't get sucked into needing the latest gadget or the newest update to your phone or computer. You probably don't really need the upgrade.
- Learn to enjoy things without owning them. Enjoy the library, the public park, the beach. We are obsessed with owning things because if we own it, we can control it.
- Develop a deep appreciation for creation. When you really see how wonderful the things that God made

are, the things that men make don't really seem all that great.

- Don't buy on credit. When you buy on credit, you are a slave to the lender until you have paid back the debt.
- Obey Jesus' command about plain, honest speech. In Matthew 5:34-37 Jesus says "... *Swear not at all...let your yes be yes and your no be no; anything more than that is evil.*"(KJV)
- Reject anything that breeds the oppression of others. Don't buy anything you know was produced in a sweatshop; don't support companies that mistreat their workers.
- Get rid of anything that distracts you from seeking first the kingdom of heaven, even if it is a good thing like your job, family, friends, security or doing ministry for God.

# 10

## The Sub Mission

Often there comes a point in our journey where we find ourselves leveling off spiritually. We are still using all the submarines, but we see no new growth. We seem to be stuck in a rut, or worse, the storms of life hit us and we once again find ourselves tumbling around in the shallows wondering how we got there. What went wrong?

There are several possibilities, but I don't want to dwell on the problems. Instead, I want to tell you about a submarine that is designed for mid-Atlantic trench level diving. The one submarine that can burst you out of that rut and take you deeper than you have ever been before. The lack of this submarine is probably the number one reason for stagnation in the Christian walk.

What is this amazing submarine? We call it submission, which is appropriate because submission is one of the main goals of all the subs. If you like being "punny" you might say the sub mission is submission. Submission means being a willing and obedient servant, putting someone else ahead of yourself. But who are we to submit to? The answer may surprise you. James 4:7 tells us to submit to God. No surprise there, but Ephesians 5:21 tells us to submit to each other.

The Bible tells us to submit to God and other people. That combination reminds me of the great commandments Jesus gave in Matthew 22:37-39. He said, *"Love the Lord your God with all your heart, soul, mind and strength. This is the first and greatest commandment, and the second is like unto it. You shall love your neighbor as yourself..."*(NIV) So according to the Bible, we are to both love and submit to God and others. I believe that love and submission are the same thing.

Our society teaches us that love is an emotion. If you get sweaty palms, your heart beats funny, and you feel all warm and squishy inside when you're around someone, then that means you love them. When the feeling passes, then you don't love them anymore. No wonder the divorce rate is so high in this country. Love isn't a feeling.

Love is a decision that you make to put someone else's needs ahead of your own. Almost everyone is familiar with John 3:16, which tells us that *"God so love the world that He gave His only begotten son..."*(KJV) He decided to put our needs ahead of His needs.

If God's love was an emotion, He never would have given His son to die. What kind of emotion would induce you to voluntarily watch your son be murdered? God's love was His decision to put us ahead of Himself. Sounds an awful lot like submission. That's also why Jesus said in John 14:15, *"If you love me, keep my commandments."*(NIV) Our love for Jesus is manifest through our obedient submission.

When you understand what love is, it helps you to make sense of a very misused verse. Ephesians 5:22 says, *"Wives submit to your husbands."* (NIV) That is where many men stop and they use this text as a club to get their wives to do what they want. But if you read through the rest of the chapter, you will find it talks a lot about husbands loving their wives.

If love is the same thing as submission, then I could paraphrase what Paul is saying as *"Wives submit to your husbands, and husbands submit to your wives."* I believe this is exactly what he is saying because the entire section is an example of what he was trying to tell us in verse 21 which was, "Submit to each other."

When you understand what Biblical love is, some of Jesus' commands begin to make more sense. When Jesus tells us in Matthew 5:44 to love our enemies, He isn't saying we should have warm fuzzy feelings for them. He is telling us that we should try to find ways to make them happy; we should work towards what would be best for them. We put their needs ahead of our own. We can't work up good feeling for someone who has hurt us, but we can work for their good in spite of our feelings. Our motivation for doing so, is because that is exactly what God did for us.

While we were His enemies, He sent His son to die for us. The good feelings that motivate our actions towards our enemies are the good feelings we have toward God because He first loved us. If we love others as an act of service and gratitude to God, then we are able to do what would be impossible for us without God.

If you really begin to understand this concept and to live it out, it will transform all of your relationships including your relationship with God. Decide right now that you are going to demonstrate love for your family even when you don't feel like it. In fact, you should put them ahead of yourself especially when you don't feel like it, especially when they don't deserve it. If you will consistently do this, you will find that it will dramatically improve your relationships.

Most people will gladly put someone else ahead of themselves when they have those loving feelings. But when the feelings are gone, so is their demonstration of unselfishness. However, when you unselfishly do something for another person, it ignites in them that loving feeling. Then they are motivated to do something for you. You can't set out to do something for someone so that they will return the favor; that isn't love, it is manipulation. Unfortunately, that is the level that many relationships have sunk to in our culture.

Disappointingly, Christian marriages don't have a better track record than any other marriages. I know this is going to sound off topic, but stick with me. When you go to McDonald's and you order combo number 2 or whatever your favorite meal is, they always ask you the same question. "Do you want to supersize that order?" You can be satisfied with just what you asked for, and they will give it to you. But, they want to offer you something more.

Jesus said I have come that you might have life and have it more abundantly. Now, you can be satisfied just living the same normal kind of life as everyone else, or you can take the abundant life Jesus offers.

Do you want your marriage to be like everyone else's or would you like God to supersize it for you? If you want the abundant life, you have to become a disciple of Jesus. Mark 8:34 says *"If anyone wants to be my disciple, he must deny himself, take up his cross and follow me."* Denying yourself means that you are going to give up trying to get what you want. Taking up your cross means putting to death your rights to live your own life, and submitting to God's sovereign reign over your life.

We often think that our happiness is based on getting what we want, but God stands that on its head and tells us we must deny ourselves so we can have the abundant life He wants for us. Philippians 2:3-9 summarizes all this better than I could.

*"Do nothing out of selfish ambition or vain conceit. Rather, in humility, value others above yourselves, not looking to your own interests but each of you to the interests of the others. In your relationships with one another, have the same mindset as Christ Jesus: Who, being in very nature God, did not consider equality with God something to be used to his own advantage; rather, he made himself nothing by taking the very nature of a servant, being made in human likeness. And being found in appearance as a man, he humbled himself by becoming obedient to death — even death on a cross! Therefore,*

*God exalted him to the highest place and gave him the name that is above every name."* (NIV)

In other words, to be exalted in heaven, you have to submit to God and to others even to the point of death. You give up all rights to yourself, and God will raise you up and give you honor.

So how exactly do we go about submitting? Do we just carry around a white flag with us or what? There are two parts to submitting. Submitting to others and submitting to God. Submitting to others is closely connected to another submarine called service. We will examine that one in a later chapter.

Submitting to God involves surrendering control of our life over to our creator. There are three areas God especially wants to have control over; your time, your treasure, and your talents. If you think about it, your time really is your life. The way you spend your time is the way you are spending your life. If you waste time, you are wasting your life. God wants total and complete control over your time. It is so important that God created a submarine to help teach us how to give Him control of our time. We are going to talk about that submarine in the next chapter.

Your treasure is all the things that you have accumulated in exchange for your time. If you lived alone in the world, you would only possess the things that you had used your time to make, find or grow. Since we don't live alone, we use our time to make things that other people can use. In exchange, people give us money, which is really just a convenient way of representing our time and effort. We then use that money to buy things other people have used their time to make. So, if time is your life and money is what we trade for our time, then your treasure is what you trade your life for.

God asks you to give up your life, to deny yourself. In other words, God asks us to trade our life for Him, but the world tells us to trade our life for treasure. You can't do both, either you will live for God or you will live for money. Giving up some of our treasure is the practical way that we deny ourselves.

Tithing and giving to help others frees us from the stranglehold that money puts on our life. Giving your money is really a way of giving ourselves. So that is one way that we can give ourselves to God. We can't send our money up to heaven, so all we can do is give our money to support God's purposes here. When we do that, God looks on it as if we had given the money to him.

Our time and treasure together represent our life. God wants us to give everything we are to Him. He wants to have total control of our time and our finances. He also wants us to give him control of our talents. Your talents are what you do with your life. The temptation is to tell God what we are going to do for Him with our talents. God wants us to submit our talents to Him to use or not use as He sees fit.

For example, when I got excited about church planting, I just knew that was how I should use my talents for God. But when I tried to do it, I got shut down until God brought me to the place where I finally said, "God you can use me or not use me as you want." If you want me to just use my talents in some small corner and not church plant, it's up to you. After I submitted my talents to God in this way, He arranged circumstances and he brought me into church planting. It had to be on His terms; He has control of my talents and how I will use them, not me.

God wants total control of every aspect of your life. He isn't satisfied with 90% or even 99.99% like Ivory soap. God demands total and complete surrender. Psalm 37:4 says "*Take delight in the Lord, and he will give you the desires of your heart.*" (NIV) Some people read this and think, "Great! If I'm a Christian, God will give me what I want.'

What this really means is that if we recognize God as the true source of our happiness and seek Him, then God will give us what we are searching for — Himself. If you want the abundant life, get rid of anything that keeps you from wholehearted surrender to God. Make an intimate relationship with God the sole purpose of your existence and you will find that He really is all you need.

There is a well-known story about a chicken and a pig that I enjoy telling. The chicken and the pig both lived on a farm owned by farmer Gray. Farmer Gray took good care of the animals and they loved him. One day the pig said to the chicken: "*oink, oink, oink.*" For those of you who don't speak pig that means: "*Farmer Gray is so good to us, we should do something nice for him.*" The chicken responded: "*bok, bok, bok*". Which means: "*I know. We could do him up a big breakfast with bacon and eggs.*" To which the pig responded: "*That's easy for you to say, for you, it's a small sacrifice but for me, it's total commitment.*"

God isn't asking you to sacrifice for Him; He wants nothing less than a total commitment. Are you ready to take the plunge? Submit totally to God, and go deeper than you ever imagined? I can guarantee you the road won't be easy, but it will be an adventure, and it will be worth it.

# 11

# Sabbath

In this chapter, I am going to let you in on God's secret for rescuing you from a life of busyness, stress, and anxiety. In the last chapter, I wrote that submitting to God involves giving Him control of our time, our treasure and our talents.

Our time is our life; the way you spend your time is the way that you are spending your life. In this chapter, we are going to examine a submarine that God gave us to help us learn to submit our time to Him. I am convinced that all our worries and stress are based on our need to control our lives instead of letting God be God in our lives.

The Bible teaches that you are a slave to whatever god you serve. An atheist may fool himself into believing that he doesn't serve any god, but the truth is that we all serve something. Whatever is most important to you is going to control your life and demand all your spare time.

If money is most important to you, then you will constantly be obsessing about work. If power is what you seek, then your time will be consumed with scheming up ways to get more of it. If pleasure is all you live for, then you will be constantly obsessed with your next hit of drugs, or your next sexual encounter. Sin takes many forms and we could probably spend all day giving examples of how it controls us. The bottom line is either you are going to be controlled by sin or you are going to be controlled by God.

The problem is, submitting to God isn't a one-time thing, it is something that we have to do continually. The story of the Israelite nation leaving Egypt parallels our story. They were slaves in Egypt. They didn't have any choice about how they spent their time; they were forced to work. We are used to hearing God quoted as saying through Moses: "*Let my people go*", but what he actually said was "*Let my people go that they may worship me*". Exodus 8:1 (NIV) Every time he says, "*Let my people go*" he adds the phrase "*that they may worship me.*" It used to bother me because it seemed like God, or at the very least Moses, was being dishonest. It sounded to me like they were asking pharaoh to let the Israelites go out to the desert and worship God, then they would come back.

Eventually, I realized that what God was saying is the Israelites could not worship Him as slaves. Worshipping God involves submitting ourselves to Him. Jesus made it clear that you can't serve two masters. (Matthew 6:24) Before we submitted our lives to Jesus, we were in spiritual Egypt. We were slaves to our sin. We couldn't worship God until He had freed us from our sin.

When you gave your heart to God and passed through the waters of baptism, you were purified of your sin and you were free to worship God for the first time in your life. The Israelites passed through the waters of the Red Sea and their former taskmasters were drowned. They were free to worship God for the first time in their lives. Unfortunately, even though they were free, they still acted like slaves. In fact, repeatedly you find them talking about going back to Egypt. In the same way, we so often still act like we are slaves to sin, and often find ourselves heading back to spiritual Egypt.

God wants to have complete control of your life and your time. Work, money, pleasure, recognition — these all have a place in our life. The problem starts when one of those things begins to take center stage in our life, usurping the place of God. That is the subtle nature of sin; it can take anything, even good necessary things and turn them into false gods.

Therefore, God gave us a tool that can help act as a reset button. It is called Sabbath. It is a day that is set aside upon which no work or selfish pleasure can make any claim. It is set aside only for God's purposes. When you experience Sabbath rest, it puts the rest of your life into perspective; it reveals when those false gods have begun to rule in your life.

Sabbath rest is not something that you do. It isn't like taking a nap. Sabbath rest is something that you enter. We don't just rest; we enter God's rest. Hebrew 4:9-11 says, *"There remains, then, a Sabbath-rest for the people of God; for anyone who enters God's rest also rests from his own work, just as God did from His. Let us, therefore, make every effort to enter that rest, so that no one will fall by following their example of disobedience."* (NIV) Notice that it says those who enter God's rest also rest from their work; not that they rest from their work and enter God's rest. The order is very important.

We enter God's rest by faith in His son. The Jews kept a Sabbath by abstaining from work, but they failed to enter His rest. We must first enter His rest by faith. We do that by totally submitting to Him. We should do that today — whatever day that happens to be when God finds you — don't delay. After we have entered God's rest, we will also rest from our work. Why? Because we are submitted to God and we are following His rhythms.

Sabbath isn't just about one day of the week; it is meant to reorient your daily life. Sabbath is God's gift to a tired, stressed out world. It is a portal into eternity. It is a tutor to teach you the rhythms of God. When you go back and look at the creation story you notice that each day it says that the evening and the morning made up each day. It always lists the evening first. Evenings are for rest and restoration, days are for work and productivity. So, in God's way of doing things, we rest first and we work from our rest. The world works until they are exhausted and then rests. We desperately need to learn God's rhythms for life.

As an aspiring musician, rhythm is my Achilles' heel. People that don't know me very well will say silly things like, "You just got to feel it." People who know me well don't say that. Instead, they show me where I am going wrong and how it is supposed to go. The problem is that I feel the music really well. I really get into it. But then I sometimes get so into it that I just can't wait to start the next phrase and I come in a count or two early.

Other times I am feeling it so much that I just want to hold that note out or add a little "shoo, wop, bop," which, of course, adds extra beats to the song. It works fine when I am the only one singing, but when I am playing with others and they don't all feel the same thing I do, it doesn't work. I find that it really helps when I am playing with a strong drummer who can emphasize the downbeats. It is like being able to hear the heartbeat of the music.

I believe that many people live lives of chaos and stress because they fail to hear the steady heartbeat of God. Do you feel His heartbeat? Does your heart beat in rhythm with His or are you living by the beat of your own drum? If you find your life is full of anxiety, busyness, and stress, then you need the submarine of Sabbath to come into your life as the steady downbeat that will get you back into sync with God's rhythm.

Exodus 20 tells us that God blessed the Sabbath day and sanctified it. The root word for sanctified in Hebrew is betrothed. The Bible says that we are the bride of Christ. The Sabbath is a mark of our betrothal; it's like a weekly date with Jesus. We should approach it with the same excitement and anticipation that we would a special anniversary celebration with our spouse.

So how do we honor Sabbath? What are practical steps we should take to use this submarine to go deeper with God? First, you must have a heart that is submitted to God. To try honoring Sabbath without first submitting to God is to fall into legalism.

Second, make the commitment that God is going to have complete control over all your time. Then you can use Sabbath as a tool to teach you to submit to God's priorities all the time. Isaiah 58:13-14 says, *"If you call the Sabbath a delight and the Lord's holy day honorable, and if you honor it by not going your own way and not doing as you please or speaking idle words, then you will find your joy in the Lord, and I will cause you to ride on the heights of the land and feast on the inheritance of your father Jacob..."* (NIV)

This text is teaching us the great paradox of submission to God. If we don't do what we want to do on the Sabbath, if we instead keep it the way God wants us to, then we will have joy.

This is a truth not just for Sabbath, but for all of life. As Jesus said, *"He who finds his life shall lose it, but he who loses his life for my sake shall find it."* Matthew 10:39 (NIV) The Sabbath can act as a tutor to teach us this lesson. When you relinquish control of the Sabbath hours, refusing to work to support yourself or to pursue the things that you want to do, you soon discover that God is true to His word and you receive the abundant life He wants for you. This gives you the courage to submit to God in the rest of your life.

The third step is to make the decision that you are going to honor Sabbath regardless of the consequences; that you are going to submit to God and not to anyone else.

The fourth step is to tell other people about your decision. Be prepared for opposition. Doing something nonsensical just because God asks you to is an affront to most people's sensibilities. Even if it doesn't affect them, people will often be upset by this because it messes with the way they understand the world.

Fifth, on the Sabbath, don't do the things that you have to do. Instead, do the things that refresh your Spirit. This will be different for everyone. For some people working in the garden is a drudgery, for others a delight. Some people feel drained after socializing with a large group, for others it is invigorating. For one day, forget about your to-do list and do the things that renew you.

This is not the same thing as just doing whatever you want. I enjoy playing video games. I rarely play them however because I find them addictive. I could easily spend a whole day playing a game and I might even want to do that, but playing video games doesn't renew me. When I am done, I feel empty and zapped of strength. I don't believe I have ever heard God speaking to me while I was playing video games. They would be a terrible Sabbath activity for me.

SCUBA diving, on the other hand, requires a lot more physical exertion than playing video games, but when I am done, I feel renewed and refreshed. I have often had great conversations with God while SCUBA diving. SCUBA diving is a great Sabbath activity for me.

Jesus was refreshed by sharing the good news with people. After he talked with the woman at the well, the disciples tried to get him to eat, but he told them he had already had his fill. Just doing God's will renewed Him so much, he didn't even need to eat. If Jesus truly lives in us, then one of the most refreshing things we can do is share our faith with someone else. Witnessing for God is a great Sabbath activity for anyone.

This is the sixth step for keeping the Sabbath; use the day for sharing your faith. When we do this, it gives the opportunity for others to be renewed when they accept Jesus. The Sabbath is all about renewal. That is why it was Jesus' favorite day to heal on. The Pharisees got really upset because Jesus was breaking their rules about Sabbath. They had over 3,000 of them. They thought the Sabbath was all about rules.

*Sabbath*

The seventh step for keeping the Sabbath is to remember that the Sabbath is about relationships, not rules. When I tell people that I honor the Sabbath, I often get the response, "*You don't have to keep the Sabbath; you aren't saved by keeping the law.*" I tell them that's like saying, "It's your birthday; you don't have to open presents." I don't have to keep the Sabbath. I know that I am saved by the blood of Jesus Christ. Because I am saved, I want to obey God's commands, I want to live on His rhythms, I want to know Him better. Keeping the Sabbath helps me to do all those things.

The Sabbath has been one of the greatest blessings in my life. It is a day each week that God has prepared for me as a special date between Him and I — a day of betrothal, celebration, and renewal. I get to enter the rest of God. It restores my soul and refocuses my attention on Him. It allows me to slip into the rhythms of eternity and away from the chaos and clamor of my busy life. The Sabbath is all about relationships, it renews my relationship with God, my family, my friends, and my church. More than almost anything else, the Sabbath is the submarine that has been most responsible for helping me to get below the waves of life and into the stillness of the deep.

Think of the Sabbath as God inviting you to dance with Him. He desires great intimacy with you, but you must get onto His rhythms. Learn to work out of your rest in Him instead of resting from your work. Learn to put aside worry, stress, and the need to take care of yourself and trust Him.

# 12
# Putting it all together

As we come to the end of this book, I want to leave you with some thoughts on how you can put the submarines into use in your life. If you merely read this book and don't change anything you do on a daily basis, then you wasted your time. If you want to change your life, you must change something that you do every day. It has been said that first you form your habits and then they form you.

I think sometimes people struggle to change their life and don't know why it is that they work hard, but nothing ever changes. They don't realize that before they can change their circumstances, they need to change themselves. To change themselves, they must change their habits.

The submarines are tools that can transform your character, but only if you do the work to actually make them into habits. Merely reading about them, or even trying them sporadically will not change your life. If you really want to learn to go deep with God, you must learn to make the submarines part of your daily life. This chapter will give you some practical advice on how to put what you have been learning into practice.

First, don't try to implement all the submarines at once. You will be overwhelmed, and it is not possible to change so many habits in your life at one time. I recommend that you choose one or two to focus on for a period of time. It takes around 60 days to really form a new habit. However, it may take a year or more to really become proficient at something that you are just starting to learn.

Be patient with yourself; your greatest growth will likely happen as you struggle and continually try things that are difficult for you. Don't expect that you are going to be good at meditating, praying, or any of the other submarines the first hundred times you try them.

Anything worth doing is worth doing poorly until you learn to do it well. When you first tried to walk, you fell down multiple times. I have never met you, but I know that is true. How do I know it? Because everyone fell down a lot while learning to walk. That is how we learn. If you had given up because you weren't good at it initially, think about how restricted your life would be today.

You will also find that some of the submarines seem to come naturally to you and that you see real spiritual growth happen almost immediately by implementing them in your life. This is encouraging and it's tempting to just concentrate on those submarines and forget the others. If you do that, however, your spiritual life will eventually plateau. It is by continually struggling and pushing forward with the areas where you are less comfortable that you will keep your spiritual life from stagnating.

For more than five years, I struggled to use spiritual journaling as a tool for my spiritual growth. I would try and do it because I knew it could be helpful for me. To be honest, sometimes I would journal just because I felt like I should or because it was the "spiritual" thing to do. I would journal for a few days and then forget about it, and not pick it up again for several months. Then I would get really motivated and journal almost every day for a month or so and then I would forget about it for six months.

One day, I was trying to journal and I began to sense that God was speaking to me. I began to write down the impressions I was getting. As I wrote, the impressions became more clear and I was able to write even more. Suddenly, what had been a dry, boring exercise had become a living connection with God. I couldn't wait to try journaling the next day.

I have continued to journal almost every day since that experience and find it to be one of the most rewarding and

*Putting it all together*

enlightening things that I do. I still have periods of time where my journaling becomes dry and I struggle to hear God's voice, but as I have continued to keep doing it, those times have become less and less frequent.

Journaling is one of the most fulfilling parts of my devotional time with God. I am convinced that it is because I kept trying even though it was clear to me I had no aptitude for it. I believe that our biggest breakthroughs come not in the areas of our natural strengths and affinities, but in the areas of our greatest weaknesses and dislikes. When God breaks through to us in those areas, I think it is easier for us to recognize His hand in it, because we know that we don't have any talent in that area. Even if we normally wouldn't enjoy an activity, when God's presence is there, suddenly everything is fresh and new.

So how do you go about forming the good habits that you want to have and get rid of the bad habits that would keep you enslaved? There are seven steps that I follow when I want to make important changes in my life. This isn't a magic formula, but it is effective if you will faithfully work the plan.

Step one is to pray and ask God to take control of this area of your life. In Matthew 26:41 Jesus said, "*Watch and pray so that you will not fall into temptation. The spirit is willing, but the flesh is weak."* (NIV) In other words, just wanting to change isn't enough; our flesh is too weak to be able to follow through and do what needs to be done. It is only by praying and relying on God's power that we can hope to change.

The second step is to bring the long-term results into the short-term by learning how to keep score. One of the problems we face when trying to change our habits is that the short-term feelings and the long-term results are at odds with each other. Smoking a cigarette can make you feel good in the moment even as it is killing you long-term. Galatians 6:7-8 states, *"Do not be deceived: God cannot be mocked. A man reaps what he sows. Whoever sows to please their flesh, from the flesh will reap destruction; whoever sows to please the Spirit, from the Spirit will reap eternal life."* (NIV)

The only problem with this reaping principle is that there is a delay between the sowing and the reaping. If we want to reap a good harvest, we have to learn to keep track of what we are sowing so that we are looking forward to the harvest and aren't surprised when the consequences of our actions catch up with us. You need to have a score card for whatever area you are working on changing.

For instance, if you are trying to eat healthy, put a big chart on the fridge and every time you eat a meal of only healthy food, draw a smiley face. If you eat something unhealthy, draw a frowny face. Just the act of keeping track of what you are doing can be a powerful motivator to help you change your behavior. Be creative with how you keep score, have fun, and make it a game, but make sure that you do it.

The third step in changing your habits is to fail forward by learning and practicing. Everyone messes up and fails sometimes. Those who eventually succeed are the ones who see their failures as opportunities to learn and grow. When you do that, you are actually failing forward. In other words, you fell, but you still moved closer to your goal 1 Corinthians 10:13 states, "*No temptation has overtaken you except what is common to mankind. And God is faithful; he will not let you be tempted beyond what you can bear. But when you are tempted, he will also provide a way out so that you can endure it.*" (NIV)

This means there is always a way that we can get through anything without messing up and sinning and falling short. When you mess up, decide how you should have handled things. Then you need to actually practice doing that. It might be just mentally practicing it, but if it is possible, actually going and physically doing things the way you should have is very helpful.

The fourth step in changing a habit is to find people who are either good at what you want to be doing, or who have the same goals as you do and surround yourself with these people. Recruit a friend or family member to work on the same submarine that you want to add to your regular rhythms or find someone who does it well and ask them to mentor you.

When you feel like you are all alone in something, it seems so hard and lonely. But when you have other people encouraging you, cheering for you, holding you accountable when you mess up, and struggling with you, then suddenly life is a lot more fun and things just seem easier.

The fifth thing you may need to do to change some of your habits is to spend less time with people who are going to cause you to mess up. 1 Corinthians 15:33 states, *"Do not be misled: Bad company corrupts good character"*. (NIV) I am not saying that you should remove all lost people out of your life; that would destroy your witness. However, if you are going to bring more positive people around you to help you develop positive new habits, you may

*Putting it all together*

need to spend less time with the people who are just reinforcing habits that you don't want in your life.

My sixth suggestion for making these submarines into part of your habitual practices is to reward yourself for doing the positive things that you dislike doing. If you don't enjoy studying scripture for instance, you might decide that if you study every day for a week then you will spend an afternoon going to a movie and out to eat with your friends. It is even stronger motivation if you put the scheduled reward on your calendar. Call your friends and set up the day out, but let them know that you can't go if you don't follow through on your commitment. If you feel like you might lose out on something you already have planned, then you are even more motivated than if you are just trying to reach a reward. Plus, your friends will bug you all week to do what you are supposed to do so you can go to the movie with them.

My final suggestion for putting the submarines to work in your life is to change your environment. You want to keep good things close and convenient and bad things distant and difficult. Get rid of anything that reminds you of something you want to change. Put up scriptures and reminders of what you do want. Put reminders on your mirror, on the dashboard of your car, or your front door to nudge you into taking the actions you need to do to make changes in your life today. If you are struggling to give up junk food, don't have any in your house or at least put it where you need a ladder to get to it.

A final thought before we part ways: Don't limit yourself to just the submarines in this book. God can use anything to help you grow in Him. Pay attention to the things God is trying to teach you through your circumstances, especially the painful ones. God does some of His best work in us when we are suffering, but we learn a lot more if we are looking for it and are even eager to see how God will use our pain to grow us.

As I write this final chapter I am in bed with a broken hip, broken ribs and a broken arm from a rock climbing accident. I have been learning so much from God! I am already thinking I will have to start on another book to share everything with others. I am convinced that God is always speaking to us, but He speaks the loudest through pain.

When this accident happened, I knew I had a choice to make. I could wallow in my misery or I could praise God and get excited for what God was going to teach me. I am choosing to praise God and grow through this experience. I pray that you will do the same. As

*Putting it all together*

you do, all of life will become your submarine of faith, taking you closer to God.

# Make a Difference

I hope you have found this book helpful and that you are well on your way to the intimate relationship with Jesus that you dreamed of. If that is the case, would you take a couple of minutes to help someone else to discover these tools as well? If even one person found this book because of your recommendation and was able to connect with God, wouldn't that be great! Here are a couple of things you can do:

1) Visit the listing for this book on Amazon and leave a review. It may seem that there are a lot of reviews already, but every review counts. Recent reviews will ensure that Amazon continues to show the book to people who may benefit from it.
2) Share your recommendation with your friends and church family.
3) Post your recommendation to Social Media.

# About the Author

Timothy Jemly is an author, pastor and church planter with a passion for helping people cultivate a deeper relationship with God. During his senior year in high school, his mother passed away leaving him broken and hungry for deep relationships. He turned to God to fill that need and found out the tools he had been taught for connecting with God were insufficient for the depth he desired. What started as his personal desire to know God better has turned into a lifelong quest to share with others the things he learned. He has taught thousands of people the blueprint he ultimately discovered for developing intimacy with God.

Timothy lives in Jacksonville, Florida, with his wife Amber, and his daughter Lucia. He recently planted Coastal Christian Fellowship, which he pastors. He is a sought-after speaker and spiritual coach. If you would like to connect, you can email him at TimothyJemly@gmail.com

# Endnotes

---

[i] Rice, Wayne. <u>More Hot illustrations for Youth Talks.</u> P. 77

    Zondervan Publishing House, 1995.

[ii] Lewis, C.S. <u>Mere Christianity</u>

    HarperCollins, 1952.

[iii] Tozer, A. W. <u>The Pursuit of God</u> p. 9

    Wing Spread Publishers,